LEFTY'S FAVORITE
FLY-FISHING
WATERS

LEFTY'S FAVORITE FLY-FISHING WATERS

Lefty Kreh
and
Harry Middleton

THE LYONS PRESS
Guilford, Connecticut
An imprint of The Globe Pequot Press

To buy books in quantity for corporate use
or incentives, call **(800) 962–0973, ext. 4551,**
or e-mail **premiums@GlobePequot.com.**

The Lyons Press is an imprint of The Globe Pequot Press

10 9 8 7 6 5 4 3 2 1

Printed in China

Photographs copyright © by
R. Valentine Atkinson (pages 2, 64, 148, 156/7)
Cathy and Barry Beck (pages 12, 23)
Lefty Kreh (pages 34, 74/75)
Tom Montgomery (page 90)
Jim Teeny (page 9)

ISBN 1-59228-494-9

Library of Congress Cataloging-in-Publication Data is available on file.

CONTENTS

INTRODUCTION

Now, why should Lefty Kreh presume to tell you where to fish? Well, for one thing, I'm a lucky guy. For almost 40 years now, I have been able to spend most of my time fly fishing all over the United States, either actually doing it, or talking and writing about it; and most of the time, getting paid for it, too!

It hasn't all been wine and roses, of course. Like any serious fly fisherman, I have had my share of river washouts, sun-bright salmon days, cloudy bonefish skies, fishless days and busted trips. But on balance, it's been a great life, this life of a fly-fishing professional, and if the Big Man gave me another chance, I'd ask for a second helping.

And to be an American fly-fishing professional, that's good luck squared! Because when you think about it, even with the loss of our eastern seaboard Atlantic salmon fishery (which we are slowly regaining), *Americans have the very best fly fishing in the world.* Think about it: trout, smallmouth bass and shad in the Northeast and Middle Atlantic; largemouth bass in the South; great angling for all kinds of freshwater fish in the Midwest and West; Pacific salmon and steelhead in the Northwest; plus our two fabulous national aquariums for which we are envied by fly fishermen all over the world: the huge freshwater aquarium we call Alaska, and our unique saltwater aquarium of Florida and the Florida Keys.

We have thousands of rivers, streams, lakes, ponds, and lagoons in the United States. So to choose just a few waters from that vast array — and as you will see, I have chosen to discuss just over 40 — leaves me open to the obvious criticism that an approach like this can't begin to cover all the great fisheries in our huge country. That's true: it cannot and does not. It's possible, for example, that you have a favorite local river or lake that outproduces some of the waters that I have fished on.

But a man can report only what he knows, based upon his personal experience. And there's no way, even in 40 years of fly fishing, that I could even sample — much less fish repeatedly — all of this country's great fly-fishing waters. But in that time, I have been privileged to fish almost all of the American waters that are traditionally regarded as being our very best, and to have fished them many times. From that number, I have picked my favorites. I hope, if they are not already favorite waters of yours, that they will become so in the future.

One further word of introduction. This book does not intend to be an encyclopedia. A complete exposition of all the information available about the rivers and watersheds I will be discussing would literally take thousands and thousands of pages. Entire books have even been written about some of them. So what is my purpose? And why should you want to include this book in your own fly-fishing library?

Well, my judgment is that most fly fishermen, when they can find the time and money, want to travel and fish as many great waters as they can. So I hope this book will give the traveling angler sufficient information about the critical factors that will make the difference between a

Migrating sockeye salmon on the Brooks River, Alaska. ➤

busted and a successful or wonderful fly-fishing trip if he decides to fish one of my favorite waters.

Preparing the book turned out to be a considerable task. It's one thing for me to remember a great day I had on some river in Idaho 25 years ago. It's quite another, sitting today at the word processor at my home in Maryland, for me to remember, with specificity, such critical factors as the geography of the river, its access points, its fishing rules and regulations, its tackle requirements, its hatch times, and best fly patterns.

So I asked my friend, the late Harry Middleton, who contributed to some of my previous books, to co-author the book with me. After I had compiled a list of my favorite selections, together with the editorial staff at Odysseus, Harry undertook the truly massive job of research necessary so that we could present you with accurate and timely information of my favorite watersheds.

After Harry and I had compiled our original manuscript of the book, we sent our write-up on each watershed to a fly-fishing shop or fly-fishing professional in its local area, asking them to provide us with up-to-date information and to meticulously critique our draft of the book in order to insure the accuracy and timeliness of our presentation.

They did that, as I think you will see. And by way of thanking each of these individuals for the valuable assistance they gave us, I have listed their names, addresses and telephone numbers in the Appendix to the book. If you are planning a trip to one of the rivers I will be talking about, I recommend that you call one of these great professionals to obtain the latest information on hatches, flies, tackle, accommodations, etc., so you can be well prepared for a successful trip.

I would like to acknowledge the assistance and counsel of Don Causey, president and publisher of *The Angling*

Report, 9300 S. Dadeland Blvd., Suite 605, Miami, Florida 33156 (telephone 305-670-1361). Don publishes this excellent monthly newsletter for the traveling angler, which gives up-to-date information on fly-fishing destinations throughout the United States as well as overseas.

I also want to express my thanks to a number of friends who assisted us in preparing technical information for the book — Bill Hunter, Mike Michalak, Lou Tabory, Gary Borger, Diane and Chuck Rizuto, Fran Betters, Newell Steele, Bud Johnson, Val Atkinson, Jim Teeny, R. Monty Montplaisir, and Dave Whitlock.

Now to the good stuff. Here are my favorite fly-fishing waters in the United States.

OVERLEAF: *An angler lands a brook trout on New York's upper Beaverkill River.*

CHAPTER ONE

THE NORTHEAST

PENOBSCOT RIVER
Maine

Colonial fly fishers came to Atlantic salmon fishing early, with the first record of a salmon taken on a fly in America coming in 1787 on New York's Saranac River. When that salmon was taken, Atlantic salmon populations still choked many of the river systems of the Northeast and Canada's maritime provinces, thriving in the waters around Ontario, down through the massive drainage of the St. Lawrence River and as far south as the Connecticut River, which, for decades, was the most productive salmon river in America.

However, the demise of salmon in the Northeast came quickly and dramatically, as more and more rivers were dammed, polluted by sprawling industry. In less than a century, the Atlantic salmon populations in American waters were near extinction.

In an effort to protect and preserve the small remaining populations of salmon, as early as the late 1940s the state of Maine began a statewide program to restore salmon populations to at least some of its native waters. Maine's efforts have, in turn, been embraced by several other New England states, especially Connecticut, Vermont, and New

Hampshire, which are trying to clean up more than 400 miles of the Connecticut River, hoping that salmon can be introduced and again survive and thrive there.

To date, though, Maine remains the only region in America where fly fishermen can try their skills against riverine Atlantic salmon. Among the Maine rivers now officially labeled salmon rivers are the Narraguagus, the Machias and East Machias, the Union, Sheepscot, Pleasant, and Dennys rivers.

And surely the most famous and challenging of these renewed salmon waters is the big, powerful Penobscot River, the most provocative and productive Atlantic salmon river in the United States.

It has been only twenty years since there were no salmon left in the deep, dark waters of the Penobscot. However, by the late 1970s, Maine's restoration project on the river reported that the Penobscot held almost a thousand Atlantic salmon, of which nearly 200 had been taken by rod and reel. A decade later those numbers had increased considerably, with the river's population of the species rising to nearly 3,000 salmon. Today, the Penobscot continues as the nation's most prolific and healthiest Atlantic salmon river.

The Penobscot meanders through southeastern Maine, roughly between Bangor and Brewer. A big, often powerful river, the Penobscot is wide, from 200 to 300 yards across. Even so, the river's salmon can be fished from the banks, or from drifting canoes or jon boats. Fly fishermen wanting to wade the river should remember the river's icy power and its depth. Chest waders are a must on the Penobscot; nothing less.

The salmon runs on the Penobscot usually get under way in May, early on in the month. Peak fishing periods on the river come in early to mid-June, once the water has

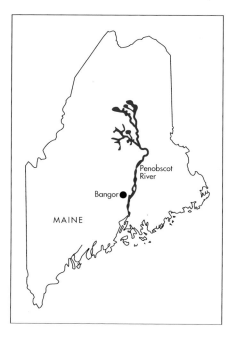

warmed a little. The salmon fishing remains good and strong through the cool days of early summer, falling off only after the waters of the Penobscot have warmed to a temperature of 65 degrees or warmer. Even though the river has warmed up, there are still chances of hooking a salmon late into the season, especially after a cold rain or on a cool, cloudy day. Often, the salmon will remain active in the early morning hours or after dusk, when the sun is off the water and temperatures are cooler.

Most of the proven salmon flies — the traditional hair-wing patterns, Silver Doctors, Jock Scotts, Dusty Millers, etc. — work well on the Penobscot. With the Atlantic salmon of the Penobscot, it's not so much the fly, or the gear, but an angler's patience that means the difference between fish and no fish.

The West Branch of the Penobscot, west of the town of Millinocket, is the best landlocked salmon river in North America, with most fish running from 12 to 18 inches, while a number are harvested in the four to six-pound range. The most productive area in this stretch of the river is from the Ripogenous Dam to the Nesowadnehunk dead waters. Popular and productive pools are the Big Eddie, Little Eddie, Holbrook, McKay Station, and the Steep Bank. There are many other productive pools along this 10-mile stretch of river, with many secluded spots to get away from the crowds.

The season on landlocked salmon opens on April first, with the best fishing starting about mid-May. The first hatch on this water is the Quill Gordon, followed by Hendricksons and Red Quills near the first of June, followed in turn by Pale Evening Duns. The caddisfly hatch predominates from June through September.

Streamers such as the Barnes Special, Black Ghost, Grey Ghost, and Muddler Minnow produce well, especially when smelts are in the river.

The Penobscot is also a superb watershed for smallmouth bass, particularly in the late summer and early fall as the water begins to cool.

CAPE COD, CUTTYHUNK, AND MARTHA'S VINEYARD
Massachusetts

High on many a fly fisherman's list of favorite saltwater species are striped bass. And while there are many superb striped bass fisheries around the country, certainly one of the great regions for this challenging and powerful fish is in the coastal waters of Massachusetts.

Off the east coast of Massachusetts lies the boomerang-shaped land mass of Cape Cod. Probably more big surf-caught stripers have been landed here than any other location in the world. The fly rodder will also find many five to 20-pound fish within easy casting distance.

Cape Cod Bay stretches from the tip of Provincetown to the Cape Cod Canal. From Provincetown to the cut at the end of Nauset Beach lie miles of open, ocean beach. This stretch of beach contains holes or bars harboring many good sloughs; with stripers and bluefish sometimes feeding right in the first wave. This aspect of the Cape is unique in that it has both open and sheltered waters that hold trophy-sized fish. While Pleasant Bay, located at the elbow of Cape Cod, is a location offering protected waters with the chance of big stripers, as well as great "schoolie" fishing.

At higher tides these beaches provide fine fishing both for striped bass and bluefish. In the fall, daytime schoolie fishing can be excellent. Favorite baitfish of this area are spearing, sand eels, and juvenile herring. Flies should match the size of these baits, in large and small patterns.

The little island of Cuttyhunk, which is at the outer-most tip of the Elizabeth Islands which trail away from the Woods Hole side of Cape Cod, has long been known for its heavyweight stripers. Sow and Pig Reef off the island's west side produces many sizeable fish (but this fishing is mostly from boats using conventional tackle). Surf fishing with a fly rod along the rugged shoreline is difficult, but rewarding. Fly fishing is also possible at Canapitsit Channel, as well as at the outlet to the pond at the island's northwest side.

To the southeast lies Martha's Vineyard, one of the two large islands south of Cape Cod. The Vineyard is a paradise for fly rodders, possibly the best location in New

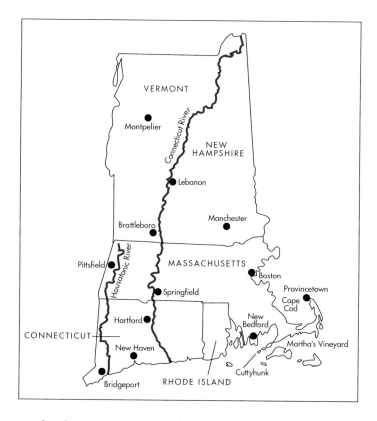

England. Striped bass, bluefish, bonito, false albacore, and weakfish invade these waters. Stripers move in first, about mid-May, followed by bluefish. The bonito arrive in mid-summer, and the albacore in early fall. September is the best month to try for all five species.

The most popular baits, again, are spearing and sand eels, as well as anchovies. These are ideal baits because they are so easy to duplicate with a fly pattern. At times, size of the fly can be important when fishing for stripers, bonito, and albacore. Flies no longer than two to five inches are best, in sizes closely duplicating the size of the baits.

There are a number of tidal ponds on the Vineyard. Two favorites are Cape Poge Bay and Menemsha Pond. Edgartown Harbor also has fine runs of bonito and albacore, but it can get crowded. At times, the ocean speeders will run right into these ponds, and night tides will find stripers up inside the shallows.

East Beach and Lobsterville are the two best fly-fishing beaches, but the entire island holds fish for the adventurous fly fisherman who is willing to devote some time to searching for them.

Perhaps the best fishing at Martha's Vineyard occurs when the bonito and albacore run the beach. Here the angler can catch an offshore fish right from the surf! The sight of a school of ocean speeders tearing into a school of baitfish in just three feet of water is unforgettable; as is the first run of a hooked fish, which leaves even the most experienced angler breathless.

UPPER CONNECTICUT RIVER

Vermont, New Hampshire, and Massachusetts

While the better trout rivers of the East often suffer, at least by reputation, when compared to the incredible trout waters of the West, there are a handful of eastern trout rivers that are in every way equal to the rivers of the West. Among them, certainly, are the tailwater section of the Housatonic, the East and West branches of the Delaware, and the renowned waters of the Beaverkill.

To these famous watersheds could reasonably be added the upper Connecticut, which begins on the Canadian border, at Fourth Lake, in Quebec province. The upper reaches of the river are marked by a series of impoundments, and move in and out of them as it flows south through New Hampshire. It winds through beautiful country, country still marked by wildness. This beauty alone makes the Connecticut one of the grand trout rivers left in the Northeast.

Below First Lake Dam and Murphy Dam on Lake Francis, the upper river is narrow pocket water that can offer some excellent trout and landlocked salmon fishing, especially when hatches are coming off the water. Hatches are not heavy or particularly regular on the Connecticut, but when they do come, the quality of the angling rises exponentially. (And I would advise you to be sure to bring plenty of insect repellent in May and June, as the area becomes saturated with black flies.)

Given the array of impoundments on the river, naturally the upper Connecticut is best known as a tailwater trout fishery. The cold water coming out of the dams keeps the river's water temperature chilly well into summer. Indeed, below the dams, often the river's average temperature will not rise above the high 50s even under an August sun.

Nearby U.S. Highway 3 allows anglers access to the stretches of the river running through the gorgeous Connecticut River Valley. Throughout this long section, the river is marked by fast water boiling over great boulder fields, long, calmer, deeper pools, and lots of pocket water holding trout.

Fluctuating water levels can and do affect trout fishing along the Connecticut. Even so, the river and its natural habitat still manage to produce a number of natural hatches, including Quill Gordons, March Browns, Hendricksons, and Blue-Winged Olives. Nymphs can also be effective in the river's deeper pools and pockets.

The best time of year to take on the Connecticut River is from mid-to-late June. And the river's trout usually continue to be around as well as active well into the fall, almost to the end of October. Most of the trout taken from the Connecticut tend to be small to average in size, but there are the occasional lunkers.

Regarding the most productive flies for the Connecticut, perhaps most important would be an ample selection of caddisflies in olive, gray, and tan (#12 to #18), Tricos and Quill Gordons (#12 to #16), and Drakes in slate, golden, and green (#8 to #12).

Knowledge of the river's water level is vital to knowing the best times to fish the upper Connecticut. The first purpose of the three impoundments between Second and Francis Lakes and south to New Hampshire's Moore Dam is to keep enough water stored at Moore Reservoir to generate electricity on demand.

Whether the turbines are on and off also greatly affects the river's trout and, consequently, fishing success. Often, when the intake of water is heavy, the best fishing on the Connecticut can be at or near the mouths of its tributaries, such as the Nulhegan, near North Stratford, and Perry Stream near the Francis Reservoir.

Some of the best trout water on the Connecticut is the eight miles of water between the towns of West Stewartstown and Colebrook. Most of the trophy-sized rainbows and browns that are taken from the Connecticut are taken from this section of the river. (It is perfect, by the way, for angling from a drifting canoe.) Other notable tributaries in the area worth fishing are the Mohawk, Clear Stream, and Indian Stream.

As the river flows further south into the state of Connecticut, trout fishing on the Connecticut drops off markedly, and the river turns into a primary habitat for other freshwater species. Fly fishermen can enjoy the day casting to smallmouth bass, pike, shad and catfish.

HOUSATONIC RIVER
Massachusetts and Connecticut

The headwaters of the Housatonic (known as "the Housy" to locals and to those that fish it regularly) gather in the stately Berkshire Mountains of Massachusetts. From there the river flows into northwestern Connecticut. Much of the course of the river is paralleled by U.S. Highway 7, which allows fly fishermen plenty of easy access.

Big and unpredictable, the Housatonic is a river with a constantly changing temper, a trout river that truly has to be watched closely, particularly because of the rapid changes in its water levels due to water releases from the Falls River Dam, which often come completely without warning. Water levels usually change at least twice daily, morning and afternoon. But since the dam's turbines are operated in response to hydroelectric power demand, there is no one predictable and inviolate schedule. The danger of the Housatonic is aggravated all the more by the fact that the best trout water along the river, a stretch of about 50 miles, is clogged with slick boulders and marked by an even slicker bottom. If chest waders are a must on Maine's Penobscot River, then a wading staff and wading cleats are highly recommended for the potentially upsetting waters of the Housatonic.

Like so many other outstanding trout rivers, the Housatonic is principally a tailwater fishery, with the best trout water found below the dam. Many of the best pools along the river are named and heavily fished. The names are legendary among local fly fishermen — Corner Hole, Dun Rollin' Pool, Split Rock, and Carse Pool.

Bruce Foster and Cathy Beck enjoy a day of trout fishing on the Delaware River. ➤

Waters both from the dam and from the river's icy tributaries keep the water temperatures of the river well within trout range from early spring until July, and fishing on the Housatonic can be most productive at that time. And even though the trout water on the Housatonic is not closed to angling at any time of the year, areas within 100 feet of the tributaries are closed during July and August, when many trout move to cooler water to escape the high temperatures of summer in the main river.

It was not so long ago that the Housatonic, like so many northeastern trout habitats, was in deep trouble. In the late 1970s, for example, the trout population in the river dropped by more than 50 percent when the state ceased stocking the water when it was determined that the trout were unfit for consumption because of PCB contamination. Most anglers simply left, believing that the Housatonic was just another dying trout river. Those that loved the river, however, fought for it, wanted to make it strictly catch-and-release, and in the end it was decided to continue stocking the river sufficiently enough to maintain it as a viable trout and recreational fishery. Brown trout were brought in from Montana's Bitteroot River, which quickly proved heartier and more adaptable than the local hatchery trout. Also, rainbow trout have been introduced to the river during the last two seasons.

Those fly fishermen who regularly fish the Housatonic believe it both looks and fishes like a western trout river. It is a big river, marked by long pools, fast shoals, swift eddies. And with the successful introduction of the Montana browns, the Housatonic has again acquired a reputation as one of the best brown trout rivers in the East.

Lately, anglers have been working the Housatonic as much for its swelling smallmouth bass population as for its trout. In recent years there has been an increase of smallmouths in the river accompanied by an equal decrease of trout. Warming of the river has likely caused this change in its character from good trout to small-mouth habitat. Also, the river's unsteady water levels have hurt the native trout while helping the smallmouth.

Streamers and nymphs generally provide the most productive angling. But there are some worthy hatches along the river, including White Flies, Black Caddis, Grannoms, and Hendricksons. For the most part, caddisflies dominate the Housatonic, especially after early June. Among the fly patterns most effective on the Housatonic are caddis pupae, turkey wing caddisflies, Little Black Caddis, Spotted Sedges, March Browns, Tricos, White Flies, Little Blue-Winged Olives, Pale Evening Duns, Alder Flies, Light Cahills and Housatonic Quills. A wide range of pattern sizes is a must (from #10 to the #18 to #26 range).

The Housatonic Trout Management Area takes in about nine miles of river from above West Cornwall downstream to Cornwall Bridge. Three miles of the river, between Cornwall Bridge to Dun Rollin' Pool, is restricted to fly fishing only. The entire management area is strictly catch-and-release.

The Housatonic is a challenging and productive trout river throughout the year. The fishing is as good in September and October as it is in late May and early June. Once the fall weather settles in, Muddler Minnows, Woolly Buggers, and Blue-Winged Olives become important flies.

LONG ISLAND SOUND
New York and Connecticut

Fish are not always where human beings are not. Perhaps one of the greatest examples of this alluring paradox is

Long Island Sound, which rings one of the most heavily populated and developed pieces of real estate on the planet. The waters of the Sound teem with gamefish, particularly great populations of striped bass and bluefish; and today the fishing on the Sound is becoming even better every year — especially for stripers — thanks to restrictions that have been placed on commercial fishing in the area.

Access to the best fishing along the Long Island side of the Sound is easy and plentiful, allowing fly fishermen to get at the fish without having to contend with boat rentals. All that is needed is a local tide chart, a good pair of waders, and a reliable map of the Sound and its shoreline.

However, public access along the Westchester, New York and Connecticut coasts can be very difficult. Shorefront homes on private property line this coast, and anglers wanting to wade from that side of the Sound are forced to concentrate at wadeable public areas such as Penfield Reef in Stamford, Connecticut.

However, boat fishing along this coast can be excellent, particularly in the fall when many of the harbors are filled with huge schools of bunkers (Atlantic menhaden). This concentration of bait lures in large blues and stripers for a frantic feast. The Sound also contains many reefs that sit just below the water at high tide, creating very productive fishing for the boat angler.

The Sound's striped bass tend to move with the schools of baitfish, so that any sign of baitfish — sand eels, butterfish, small herring, and so on — usually means that big gamefish are near at hand. Fish can also sometimes be spotted feeding on shrimp and crabs.

For bluefish, wire leaders and slow and full-sinking lines are essential for fishing Long Island Sound. Any number of saltwater flies works well in the Sound, again because striped bass, bluefish, and weakfish are not normally that finicky about what they hit, especially when they are actively feeding. Poppers work well, as does the Lefty's Deceiver in a variety of colors, the Muddler Minnow, Surf Candy, Clouser Deep Minnow, Finger Mullet, Bonito Fly, and Salt Streaker patterns.

Migrating striped bass generally begin showing up in Long Island Sound sometime in April, and the best fishing spots at that time are in the warmer water at the river mouths. For example, the area at the mouth of the Hudson River is often teeming with bass. These early bass can be young and small. As the season progresses and the waters warm, bigger adults begin to move northward along the coasts of the Sound.

Migrating bass and great schools of sand eels usually fill the Sound beginning in May. The presence of the sand eels ignites the bass, and they move in larger numbers out of the Hudson River. Also, large numbers of Chesapeake Bay striped bass begin entering the Sound at this time, especially around Montauk.

The press of the sand eels probably makes June the best month for striped bass in the Sound. Fishing is excellent on both the Connecticut and Long Island shores, with morning and evening being the most productive times of the day for taking lots of bass.

By mid-June, bluefish begin showing up in greater numbers and can be stalked in shallow water just as you would hunt for bonefish on a Florida Keys' flat.

By the end of June, the striped bass and bluefish are joined by growing numbers of weakfish, which offer the fly fisherman some challenging and exciting night fishing throughout the summer.

Stripers and bluefish (especially bluefish) hold in the Sound through the summer and early fall.

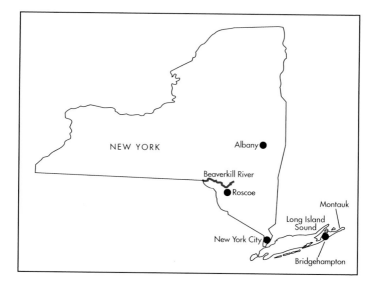

In addition, large swarms of big bluefish — snappers and alligator blues — begin showing up in the Sound in August and September, giving the angler a chance to sample what it is like to fish a true bluefish feeding frenzy, as the marauding blues chase down schools of menhaden.

Also during late August and early September, schools of bonito often enter the Sound, creating havoc for the anglers who don't realize what they've hooked into.

There can be good fly fishing throughout the winter months for schoolie bass, particularly around the area of Northport's power plant on the north shore of Long Island as the plant's water discharges create a warm-water habitat.

One of the choice sites for both striped bass and bluefish is the area around Montauk. Prime bluefish water continues offshore to nearby Block Island, which is not usually considered a part of Long Island Sound. Even so, great numbers of bluefish usually mark the waters on both sides of Long Island. Prime locations are between Montauk Point (at the lighthouse) and Block Island, the Cartwright Area and the fabled Triangle. On the Long Island side of Block Island Sound, there is Great Gull Island, Gardiners Bay, the Race, Plum Island, Gardiners Point, Pocketbook, Shagwong, Cherry Harbor, Pigeon Rip, the Sluiceway, and the Ruins.

Surf casting for blues at Montauk (on the south shore, from Dutch Plains to Montauk Point State Park) offers some of the best bluefish action in the world, especially in September and October, as the blues begin to gather in groups. At that time there is always the chance of a bluefish blitz.

When the Chesapeake runs of striped bass are on the move, the waters south of Montauk also provide some superior striper fishing, especially during the peak migratory periods in the spring and fall. At Montauk, the best time for stripers is generally after sunset, when the fish often move into shallower water.

For the angler, again the best bet at Montauk for stripers is in the surf. Surf casting along the beach at Montauk Point (at the lighthouse) is an excellent site, as is nearby Jones Reef and Dutch Plains. Again, even when surf casting, the best time for Montauk stripers is after nightfall. The best striper months here are from September through Thanksgiving into the early weeks of December.

BEAVERKILL RIVER
New York

One of the most enduring of all America's trout streams, the Beaverkill is rich in natural and angling history. Much of the character of fly fishing in America was formed along the banks and in the cold, swift waters of the Beaverkill.

Flowing through the worn and eroded mountain country of the southern Catskills, less than three hours from the crush of New York City, the Beaverkill remains one of the best and most fascinating trout streams in the eastern United States. Considering its proximity to New York City and to the relentless pressures of the modern world and all that world entails, the Beaverkill's tenacity is more than impressive. Often, it borders on the incredible.

Running down through the cool, blue shadows of the thick, beautiful Catskill forests of Sullivan and Delaware counties, the Beaverkill River flows east to west for more than 40 miles before joining with the waters of the East Branch of the Delaware River.

The Beaverkill has been a haven for fly fishermen for more than a century. The Catskills offered solitude and deep forests, along with a wide variety of vacation resorts, even in the 1870s. And, most important, the river had a deserved reputation as one of the best native brook trout rivers in the country. It was this reputation that lured anglers from around the country and put an ever increasing amount of fishing pressure on the fishery. As a result, together with the simultaneous environmental impact of heavy logging and small dams, the river's once plentiful population of native brook trout began to decline drastically. The Beaverkill was quickly becoming a trout stream without trout. Desperate not to lose the lucrative tourist dollars brought in by the fishing, the New York-Oswego Midland railroad, which carried so many New Yorkers from the city up to the resorts in the Catskill mountains, paid to have the Beaverkill stocked.

The railroad's stocking program eventually dumped more than a million trout into the river. In time, these new brown trout from Germany became the river's dominant trout species. The Beaverkill, along with Michigan's Pere

Marquette River, was among the first of the nation's premier brown trout fisheries.

By the turn of the century, the Beaverkill had regained its stature as one of the best trout rivers in the Northeast. The stocked browns not only survived; they thrived, even moving into the warmer waters along the lower stretches of the river. (There are also rainbow trout in the Beaverkill, but their numbers are small.)

Fly fishermen usually divide the Beaverkill into two distinct areas — the upper and the lower river. One of the reasons being that water temperatures vary significantly between these two sections of the river.

Below Junction Pool (where the Beaverkill is joined by the waters of Willowemoc Creek), the lower river widens and takes on size and power. This section of water, which is broad and open, can heat up quickly, with the water temperature rising during the hot summer afternoons into the 80s. Such temperatures drive the trout remaining in the lower river into the cooler, deeper water of deep spring holes and the cooler waters at the mouths of feeder streams and creeks. This entire section of the river, some 14 miles of water downstream from Junction Pool, near the town of Roscoe, flows through a narrow valley and is accessible to anglers by way of both the old and new Route 17 roadways which follow the river closely, even crossing it several times.

By way of comparison, the upper Beaverkill flows through rough mountain country, through narrow valleys thick with mature forests that shade the river, keeping its waters cool year-round. The upper section flows across a lot of privately owned land. Indeed, the only public fishing on the upper Beaverkill is along the river's headwaters (less than two miles of river) and the two and one-half miles of river upstream of Junction Pool near Roscoe.

Also, the waters of the upper Beaverkill are still brook trout water, while it is uncommon to catch a brook trout below Junction Pool (from Junction Pool downstream, the river remains a brown trout river). Also, the trout of the upper Beaverkill, both brook trout and browns, tend to be wild, while the trout of the lower Beaverkill are almost all stocked (with the notable exception of the big browns of the lower river, which I will be discussing next).

Some of the most famous trout water in the history of American fly fishing belongs to the lower section of the Beaverkill, below Junction Pool. Here are the pools that saturate so much of the rich literature of American fly fishing — Hendrickson's Pool, Cairns' Pool, Barnhart's Pool, and Wagon Tracks Pool.

It should be noted that there are two no-kill stretches of water along this lower section of the Beaverkill. The first is a mile below Junction Pool and takes in more than two miles of water. The second, which includes more than a mile of the river, is near the town of Horton. These no-kill sections of the river are open year-round. Only artificial lures can be used and all trout caught must be released and returned to the river.

While the Beaverkill's early reputation was gained because of its fine native brook trout waters, today the river is more widely known as one of the better brown trout rivers in the Northeast. It is a reputation that has held firm for more than sixty years now. The lower Beaverkill, and the nearby Willowemoc, still offer some excellent brown trout fishing, with most of the river's brown trout ranging from 10 to 16 inches. Two-pound browns in the lower river are common, and on good days the skilled angler can expect to catch from 10 to 15 trout during the months of May and June. Because despite the heavy pressure it receives year-round, the lower Beaverkill remains an extremely healthy trout river, with waters rich in insect life that serve to produce a large number of fine brown trout.

The seasons on the Beaverkill are still marked by the regular rhythm of natural insect hatches, including amazing mayfly hatches. The river's legendary Hendrickson hatch in early May, for instance, seems to always draw a crowd, and is truly an experience every fly fisherman should try to sample at least once in his life.

Much of what is now considered the tradition of American dry-fly fishing got its start on the Beaverkill River and other trout streams of the Northeast, and each year thousands of dry-fly fishermen come to this legendary water to test their angling skills.

Anglers wanting to fish as early as possible might want to start the spring on the Willowemoc, where the trout are active as early as April. Action on the Beaverkill often does not truly begin until May, with the best time on the river being later still, in the early days of June. Too, crowds on the Beaverkill usually begin to thin after the May hatches.

Given its history and its continued reputation as a first-rate trout river, the Beaverkill draws a great many fly fishermen to its waters. The crowds can be considerable, but, as is true on almost any well-known trout river, the anglers tend to gather always along the same stretches of water, the same pools. For the fly fisherman who is willing to risk a walk, to move, to try a more quiet stretch of water, there is plenty of river, plenty of room, even peace and quiet to settle even the most rattled disposition.

OVERLEAF: *An angler at Pennsylvania's Falling Spring, one of the many limestone streams of the watershed that includes the famed Letort Spring Run.*

CHAPTER TWO

THE
MIDDLE ATLANTIC

DELAWARE RIVER
New Jersey, Pennsylvania, and New York

The watershed of the Delaware River is one of the biggest in the northeastern United States, draining three of the largest and most heavily populated states in the country, New York, Pennsylvania, and New Jersey. Below its East and West branches, the Delaware is a big river, moving a tremendous amount of water. As it flows down along the boundary between New York and Pennsylvania, the river separates the Catskill mountains of New York from the Pocono mountains of Pennsylvania.

As a fishery, the main channel of the Delaware is most famous for its incredible shad fishing. Like salmon, shad are an anadromous fish, spawning in freshwater and maturing in saltwater. Shad are members of the herring family, and its three major North American species are the American shad (also known as the white shad), the Alabama shad, and the hickory shad.

Each spring shad begin to gather in huge numbers in Delaware Bay. Then as the season progresses and the waters begin to warm, these huge schools of shad will begin one of the longest river migrations of any fish in

North America. Shad will not enter the river until the water has warmed to at least 50 degrees, which is usually in early-to-mid April. Their spawning run will then last into early June, with the peak period coming in May.

The male shad, who have spent more than three years at sea, will move up into the river from Delaware Bay first, eager to spawn. The males average about two pounds. The bigger, heavier females, which follow the males upstream, average about three or four pounds. Also, the females are generally older than the males.

The number of shad making the trip up the Delaware varies, but on the average, it has been estimated that between 100,000 and 200,000 shad undertake the long journey out of Delaware Bay and up the Delaware River each season. Studies with tagged migrating shad have shown that during their spawning run up the river, the fish cover from six to 15 miles a day.

These migrating shad will run the entire length of the Delaware, more than 350 miles, to junctions where the main channel of the Delaware splits into the East Branch (into which New York's famous Beaverkill and Willowemoc Rivers empty), and the West Branch. Some shad will move into both these branches of the upper river.

What makes this yearly shad migration even more astonishing is the fact that the fish, so far, have been able to maintain their migrations despite the existence today of heavy pollution that has adversely affected certain sections of the river, especially near Philadelphia.

Despite the demise and ruin of much of their spawning grounds, shad have proved themselves, again and again, to be truly remarkable fish of incredible strength, tenacity, and endurance, moving from saltwater to fresh, through miles and miles of polluted water, over a number of other obstacles presented by the river, and finally, after a jour-

ney covering hundreds of miles, reaching the cold, deep, pools of the upper Delaware where they spawn in the waters near Tusten and Lordville.

Shad fishermen will usually start taking migrating fish near Lambertville, New Jersey, during the first or second week of April, while anglers in New York will not begin seeing the moving shad until early May. By the second week of May, shad are entering the West Branch and East Branch of the river, where they will stay until July.

During the roughly four months of the shad's spawning run, there is probably no better shad fishing anywhere than that which is available along the Delaware River. The best place for trying shad on the fly rod is along the upper reaches of the river, near the headwaters, and on the East Branch. The river is smaller and shallower here, which allows fly fishermen to wade the river more easily and to get closer to the fish.

Because these Delaware shad are fished off the bottom, most fly fishermen work the Delaware shad run with sinking lines and weighted wet flies, the most effective patterns being those developed locally for fishing the Delaware shad. However, under certain conditions, Delaware shad can also provide great dry-fly angling.

For example, in the upper reaches of the Delaware, particularly on the East Branch, shad will often rise at dusk alongside trout to feed from the surface. Compared to trout, shad are eccentric feeders with erratic appetites. And while they are not as picky as trout when it comes to flies, they are constantly on the move, so that they never rise in the same place twice. Consequently, sight fishing becomes important with shad.

Shad are big fish and in the shallow waters of the upper Delaware, they flash a beautiful shade of blue. If you spot one, there are certainly more at hand. If you can see them and get a fly in front of them, or put a cast where you think they might rise, then your chances of success are greatly increased. In late summer, a Light Cahill pattern seems to work well on Delaware shad, as does an Adams (#10 to #16). However, I believe that in dry-fly fishing for shad, pattern selection is far less important than presentation.

Mornings and late afternoons until twilight are the best times for taking shad on the fly rod.

Once hooked, they are tenacious fighters. It is not uncommon for a large shad to nearly empty a reel of backing.

There are many great areas along the Delaware where shad anglers gather each year, including, in the New York sections of the river, Port Jervis, Ten Mile River, and Barryville; and in the New Jersey sections, Frenchtown, Trenton Falls, New Hope, Belvidere, and Dingman's Ferry.

The upper Delaware and the East Branch are also superb brown trout waters. Indeed, the Delaware is considered to be one of the finest tailwater trout fisheries in the eastern United States. Nearly the entire length of the East Branch below the Pepacton Reservoir, and the West Branch below the Cannonsville Reservoir (down to where both branches join to form the main channel of the Delaware and beyond) are marked by big, smooth pools, and perfect shallow runs of faster water. Good trout fishing continues down the upper Delaware for more than ten miles, between Hancock and Callicoon, New York.

But likely the principal reason why the Delaware does not receive the acclaim it is due as a superb trout fishery is the difficulty of access to the river for anglers, notably on the section of the river that flows through New York State, where most of the land is privately owned and posted against trespass. Before planning a fishing trip to this water, it's best to check with a local source for current information on where you can gain access to the river without encountering problems.

For the fly fisherman wanting a dry-fly challenge, the trout of the East Branch are considered among the most selective wild river trout in the Northeast. But I ought to warn you, these brown trout (as well as the rainbows that inhabit this water) are wild and extremely wary and difficult to tempt, much less catch.

The lower section of the Delaware is also considered a fine smallmouth bass river.

JUNIATA RIVER
Pennsylvania

Smallmouth bass are my favorite freshwater fish, and for nearly 40 years in pursuit of the smallmouth I have been traveling to the Juniata River in Pennsylvania, not far from

Harrisburg. The Juniata is an ideal fly-fishing river. It's big enough to be fished in a boat or canoe, yet it can be waded in many areas. It is typical of the limestone rivers that thread their way through the countryside of the mid-Atlantic area of Pennsylvania, Maryland, Virginia, Ohio and West Virginia, rivers in which high mineral content enriches the watershed and creates a great habitat for hellgrammites, crayfish, and scads of minnows which grow big and fat in these rivers.

If God were to pick a perfect habitat for smallmouth bass, it would be a river similar to the Juniata (or the Susquehanna into which the Juniata flows just downstream from Clark's Ferry, or about 20 miles upstream from Harrisburg).

What would be an ideal smallmouth river? Well, it would have a rather clean, rock rubble bottom, with many ledges for bass to seek a place of ambush. It would have willow grassbeds dotting the shoreline. It would have long, deep pools to provide safety and shelter for the fish during winter's siege. And between the pools, it would have riffles where the water could tumble over the rocks, putting vital oxygen into this liquid world of bass. The Juniata (and the Susquehanna) fill the demands for such a habitat to perfection.

The Juniata is not wide, but it is a long river, traversing much of central Pennsylvania. Its headwaters are a well-known trout habitat. And near Huntingdon, Pennsylvania, a huge dam has created Raystown Lake, producing one of the best striped bass fisheries in the mid-Atlantic area, a wonderful place as well to fish for both largemouth and smallmouth bass.

Below Huntingdon, all the way to Lewistown, fly fishermen catch not only bass but also walleyes and musky which have been stocked in the fishery.

The part of the Juniata I enjoy fishing most is the stretch of the river approximately 40 miles long flowing from Lewistown downstream to its junction with the Susquehanna. This is the cream of the smallmouth fishing on the Juniata River.

There's easy access to the river. Beginning at its mouth at Clark's Ferry, and extending for the entire distance to Lewistown, the Juniata is closely paralleled by an excellent highway, Route 22/322. This makes it easy to park in many places and walk to the river, or to use one of the boat ramps maintained by the Pennsylvania Boat and Fish Commission at bridge crossings. Traveling downstream from Lewistown to the mouth of the river, you will find that there are boat ramps and take-out points along the Juniata at Macedonia, Cuba Mills, Mifflintown, Mexico, Thompsontown, Newport, and Amity Hall. The distance between these boat ramps averages about five to seven miles, so you can drift from one ramp to the next downstream ramp in a comfortable one-day float.

Also, there are numerous places on the Juniata where you can wade. One of my favorites is only a few miles from the mouth of the river, along Route 22/322, near the small community of Watts. From this position on the highway well above the river you will see long slick, shallow glides in the water. This is an ideal spot for wading and working a fly rod.

Good fly rodding for smallmouth bass on the Juniata begins in late June and runs until late October, or even into November if the fall weather remains warm. The perfect outfit is a weight-forward 8 floating line, although there are times when the bass will be deep (in early spring, late fall and during very hot periods in mid-summer). At these times, a uniform-sinking or Teeny 300-type sinking line is recommended.

Good patterns for this type fishing are the Woolly Bugger (which imitates the hellgrammite), Clouser Deep Minnow, Clouser Crayfish, Half & Half, the Red & White Hackle Fly, as well as a variety of popping bugs.

There are times during the summer when the Juniata will come alive with rising bass — mostly in the eight to 12-inch size — taking insects from the surface. At such times, a small Woolly Bugger, a nymph, or even a popper cast to a ring soon after its appearance is dynamite. But keep in mind, these are cruising fish, so you have to get your fly to the ring site soon after it has been made.

If you enjoy fishing a smallmouth river with an average width from 100 to 250 yards wide, which can be fished from a canoe or boat or by wading, then I recommend you try Pennsylvania's Juniata River on a warm summer day.

SUSQUEHANNA RIVER
Pennsylvania

While it is not a natural smallmouth bass river, with the passing years the Susquehanna has gained a reputation for being one of the better smallmouth rivers in the mid-Atlantic. The headwaters of the Susquehanna flow through gorgeous country, marked by thick woods and muggy hemlock bogs. Its tangled forests are full of wildlife. Those rivers, creeks and streams flowing off the western shoulder of the watershed move west toward the Allegheny River, while to the east, the rivers move steadily toward the great watershed of the Delaware River. And at the heart of this country of rivers is the expansive Susquehanna, flowing inexorably toward its union with the Chesapeake Bay.

The Susquehanna River is a wide-ranging watershed, moving through a great sprawl of southeastern Pennsyl-

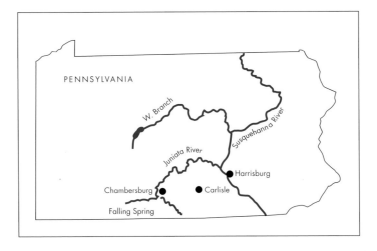

vania. Its West Branch, which flows past Williamsport, and its North Branch, which moves past Scranton and Wilkes-Barre, join to form the main channel of the river near Northumberland and Sunbury, above the mouth of the Juniata River and the city of Harrisburg.

Down where the Juniata joins the Susquehanna, the river, which feeds many dams, seems as wide and quiet as a vast system of mountain lakes. Where the river is still healthy, it still supports great populations of crayfish, which may be the favorite food of the smallmouth bass. The presence of crayfish moving in shallow water makes for nearly perfect smallmouth conditions.

Most of the smallmouth anglers who fish the Susquehanna regularly prefer that section of the river near the mouth of the Juniata. From there downstream for perhaps 40 miles, the smallmouth fishing on the river can be excellent indeed. Plenty of smallmouth are taken, as well, on the West Branch and on the North Branch above Scranton. These are truly isolated pockets of good fishing, but the river as a whole, as a system, has been severely damaged over the decades by increasing amounts of acid, brought on by acid rain, triggered by the numerous coal mines up and down the river. Though, there have been efforts of cleaning up the waters since the 1970s, and, consequently, the river is fast becoming pure again.

Smallmouth bass were first introduced to the Susquehanna in the late 1860s, when local fishermen stocked the river with bass taken from the Potomac River. (Before such stocking programs began, smallmouth bass were not native to the big rivers of the Northeast south of Canada's St. Lawrence River.)

It was here on the lower Susquehanna River that the art of taking smallmouth bass on a fly rod got its start. Tom Loving, a well-known fly fisherman from Baltimore, devised his white bucktail flies for taking Susquehanna bass and shad.

Another fly fisherman even better known for his skill with a fly rod, Ken Reid, brought the Messinger Hair Frog to the waters of the Susquehanna, where it has proved to be one of the most deadly and enduring patterns.

In addition to the crayfish, the river boasts a sizeable population of hellgrammites and minnows, which are regularly imitated by anglers with good success. And although the Susquehanna River is rich in insect life and boasts of innumerable hatches during a season, usually only the smaller-sized bass respond to them. Anglers fishing these hatches can expect to catch many smallmouth at that time.

The first of the two most important hatches on the river is the White Fly hatch, which usually occurs as early as the last week of July, and lasts for about two weeks, providing anglers with plenty of late evening action. Exact imitations of this fly may be used, of course, but it is not necessary. When feeding on the White Fly hatch, smallmouth will usually attack any small surface pattern or larger nymph.

The other notable hatch is the insect fall of a terrestrial, a flying ant, which migrates over the river to new nesting and propagation areas in the fall, usually during late September. This migration lasts only for a week, and usually peaks in just one 24-hour period. During this time the surface of the river is literally covered with ants, but most experienced Susquehanna anglers do not attempt to match the hatch then. Instead, they cast large streamers, hair bugs and cork popper patterns. The reason for this is that the carpet of ants on the water attracts small minnows out of their hiding places, and it is these small fish, not the ants, that the big smallmouths are interested in.

Although the river is ideal for shallow-draft boats — and most anglers believe they can cover more of the river and reach its better bass pools more effectively by floating — during summer low-water conditions the river can be waded in many spots. But if you do choose to wade here, keep in mind that this is a big river, as much as a half mile wide in some places, with many changes of depth that can be tricky and dangerous.

While Susquehanna smallmouths are not noted for their size, they are active and challenging, and four-pound fish are becoming more common these days as conservation measures of the Pennsylvania Fish and Boat Commission have begun to bear fruit. Size and creel limit regulations still apply on various sections of the river, so check with a local source before coming to the river.

Of course, successful conservation measures which have helped to increase the size of the smallmouth bass have also increased the fishing pressure, which in turn, may have a detrimental effect upon the river. So catch-and-release is, today, a recommended practice.

FALLING SPRING

Pennsylvania

During the late 1950s and much of the 1960s I lived in Maryland, and two of my favorite trout waters were only two hours' drive away. Both were classic Pennsylvania limestone streams — Letort in Carlisle, and Falling Spring near Chambersburg. I spent many hours there trying to deceive the wary trout.

It was a heady time for trout fly fishermen. Vince Marinaro, Charley Fox and Ross Trimmer were developing the terrestrial, a breakthrough new trout fly. Joe Brooks, my mentor and one of the most respected fishing writers of that time, urged me to seek out these men and learn not only about terrestrial fly patterns, but to become acquainted with the many limestone streams that meandered through the south-central Pennsylvania countryside.

Ross Trimmer and Jack Eschelman (the dean of Falling Spring fly fishermen) took a liking to me and I spent many hours with the two great trout fishermen as they introduced me to a number of the limestone spring creeks in the area. And of all the wonderful waters, the Letort and Falling Spring became my favorites.

Unfortunately, both streams fell on hard times. The legendary Letort is now a shadow of what it used to be. It was one of the premier trout streams in the Eastern United States. It once ran clean and clear but is now roiled by developments in the upper reaches and carp are even seen swimming in its murky waters. Falling Spring deteriorated too, and by the late 1970s I had given up fishing both of them.

But in 1988 a remarkable change and improvement began on Falling Spring. The Falling Spring Greenway, Inc. was formed with Trout Unlimited and a number of local organizations that were determined to restore it to its former greatness. Through their efforts and the cooperation of many local landowners and organizations, including the Boy Scouts, the Chambersburg Chamber of Commerce, the Guildford Township and Water Authority, and many individuals, the stream is today a wonderful place for trout fishermen.

Landowners agreed to help and allowed both fishermen access to the stream as well as help in other efforts. The Greenway purchased land when necessary, re-channeled the stream in certain areas, and built fish-friendly structures. Where once there was a marsh or stream bottom filled with sediment, there is now a narrowed, quick-flowing stream with a clean gravel bottom that is ideal for insects and spawning fish.

Falling Spring's source is a collection of small springs that contribute their cool mineral-rich waters. The consistent water temperature is perfect for the trout and the aquatic insects that live there. Thick beds of elodea and watercress provide vegetation where trout can hide and are home to huge numbers of freshwater shrimp and cress bugs — an important food source for the trout.

The stream is divided into two separate parts. The upper section (more than 2 miles) is designated as Heritage Trout Angling and is catch-and-release fly fishing only with barbless hooks. Landowners allow a 20-foot access on each side of the stream. Immediately below that is the Delayed Harvest Artificial Lures Only section where there is year-round fishing with a restriction on the number of fish anglers can keep.

For information on both sections of the stream and for suggested guides and articles written about the waters, just type "Falling Spring" on any Internet search engine.

Mike Hess, who guides on Falling Spring, gave me a complete tour of the fly fishing area. What a revelation! In various places we saw trout — some exceeding 20 inches — and Mike and others have tales of real trophies. Mike pointed out small schools of rainbows. There has been no stocking for years in the fly area and both browns and rainbows are now able to reproduce on the clean sand and gravel beds.

As for tackle, these are smart trout, so drag-free drifts are essential to success. Heavy lines crashing to the surface are not going to get you many trout. The standard rod is a 3-weight, although some fly fishermen prefer 1- and 2-weights. Long leaders are used with dry flies and tippets of 5- or 6X. I've never needed 7X or 8X tippets though some anglers insist on using these fine tippets.

The average size of dry flies and nymphs range from #14 to #24. During the colder months you can always depend upon #14– #16 cress bugs and freshwater shrimp imitations — which abound in the aquatic vegetation in prodigious numbers. Indeed, these two patterns are good throughout the year. Nymphs are always worth trying and some patterns that have been effective are: #16 Sulphurs, #18 Baetis, a #16–#18 Pheasant Tail, the Hare's Ear (my favorite) #14–#18 and don't forget to try some #14 red midge larvae. It's worth having all of these patterns with and without bead heads.

Streamers will often fool the larger fish — especially the brown trout — and among the best is the woolly bugger. While several body colors work, I prefer a body of wound peacock herl and with either a grizzly or black palmered hackle. The Zonker and Muddler will also work at times. Try two different retrieves. On a long leader cast the fly up and across the pool and then retrieve in fast jerks. Top local guide, Mike Hess, gets results by throwing the streamer upstream on a watercress or elodea bed and then slowly pulling the fly off the bed allowing it to tumble in the current like a wounded baitfish.

It was on these spring creeks that Marinaro, Fox, and Trimmer discovered the importance of terrestrials. Don't neglect crickets, hoppers, beetles, ants (both floating and sinking), and Jassids. All fish well into late fall.

Rarely does a fly fisherman lose a river of choice and get it back. But many organizations and people have contributed to restoring Falling Spring — and it is again one of my favorite trout streams. If you live anywhere nearby you should try it — you'll be rewarded.

GUNPOWDER FALLS RIVER
Maryland

There are three major reservoirs that supply Baltimore, Maryland with drinking water. One lies to the west of the city. To the north are the other two, the Prettyboy and Loch Raven reservoirs, whose dams are constructed across Gunpowder Falls River. For many years, most of the water supplied to the city was drawn as needed from Loch Raven, the reservoir closest to Baltimore. The second reservoir, Prettyboy, is situated about 14 miles upstream from Loch Raven. For many years, when the Loch Raven Reservoir needed resupplying, the gates at the dam at Prettyboy would be opened and a wall of water would rush down the Gunpowder. When enough water had been funneled to Loch Raven, the dam gates were closed.

This routine existed for years. Most of the time the Gunpowder wasn't a stream at all, but a small creek with pools, where there was so little water that in places in late summer you could jump across it without getting your feet wet. But of course, when water was needed in the lower reservoir, the river ran bank-full. So for many years the river was in either a state of drought or flood.

Despite such harsh conditions, a few trout flourished in the Gunpowder. In the fall, some wise anglers would search the tiny springs and little creeks that fed into the river, where they would find brown trout, sometimes in excess of five pounds, spawning in the trickles of water.

But around the mid-1980s, the Maryland chapter of Trout Unlimited conducted a study of the Gunpowder, and after collecting good data they convinced city authorities that if a constant flow of water were released from Prettyboy, the Gunpowder could properly replenish Loch Raven without the need of the flood/drought conditions, and be turned into a first-rate trout habitat.

The city decided to go along with the idea, and the Maryland Department of Natural Resources, which endorsed the concept, cooperated fully. The stream began having a constant water flow. Since it originated from the cold waters at Prettyboy Dam, what resulted was a tail-water fishery — and today the Gunpowder is one of the best trout streams in the entire mid-Atlantic area. No trout stream within 150 miles of Baltimore can match it.

Natural reproduction of browns was started a few years ago on the Gunpowder when eggs from Montana were seeded in man-made spawning beds. That seeding was followed by an additional seeding of small rainbows.

Since the Gunpowder meanders through a valley containing limestone strata beneath its surface, and is fed by numerous small spring branches that carry minerals into the watershed, some fantastic natural reproduction of fish has resulted. Incidentally, the entire stream — more than 30 miles of it from Prettyboy to Chesapeake Bay — has been designated as a state park, so access to the Gunpowder by the public has been assured.

A number of insects flourish in these rich waters, including mayflies, caddisflies and some stoneflies. Crayfish are plentiful and hellgrammites are beginning to do well. Minnows hide from prowling trout among the bank cover. In a 1992 study by the Maryland Department of Natural Resources, it was determined that due to the incredible natural reproduction, the portion of the Gunpowder several miles immediately below the Prettyboy Dam was beginning to rival some of the best western U.S. streams, so far as pounds per acre of trout is concerned. The survey revealed a respectable population of fish — about 1,300 trout per mile.

Approximately eight miles of the stream, from Prettyboy Dam downstream to York Road, is now a catch-and-return area with special regulations. This is by far the most productive stretch of the 13 or 14 miles of the Gunpowder fishing area, and fly fishermen have found it to be a superb place to fish for naturally reproduced trout.

Beaver have also benefitted from this constant flow of water and have created dams which, in turn, have created some dandy long, deep pools. This is especially true in the upper area of the Gunpowder, where some of the largest trout can be found.

Because it is a tailwater fishery, you can fish the Gunpowder 12 months of the year. Even during the winter months, good fly fishing can be had by fishing small nymphs (#16 to #20) or dark stonefly patterns (#16 to #20) to imitate the little black or brown stoneflies that hatch on the Gunpowder in late January or early February when the air temperature remains above 50 degrees for several days. Usually these flies are found hatching where there is a pretty good flow of water. Since the naturals flutter on the surface as they try to fly away, a down-and-across stream cast, allowing the leader to fall to the water with a little slack, is the recommended technique. Deaddrift the fly a foot or so, and then let the leader drag the imitation a few inches. Lift the rod slowly and then drop it so you can repeat the retrieve. Don't work the fly too much or you'll discourage the trout.

By late April a number of mayflies are hatching and while you can fish exact imitations, of course, you'll generally perform very well using a suggestive fly, such as an Adams Parachute (#12 to #20).

By mid-summer Blue-Winged Olives make an appearance, and they will remain most of the summer.

The best summer dry-fly fishing on the Gunpowder, however, demands the use of terrestrials. But if you are really interested in catching trout, you need to go underwater, fishing either soft-hackle patterns or nymphs (the Gold-Ribbed Hare's Ear is one of my favorite patterns). Nymphs will also work throughout most of the year. Effective sizes range from #12 to #20.

While there are 13 to 14 miles of the Gunpowder running from Prettyboy Dam to Loch Raven, the very best fishing occurs from Falls Road upstream to the dam. Most of the stream here lies in a small canyon, so there is a little effort required to fish here. But it's well worth the sweat. From Masemore Road upstream to Falls Road is perhaps the second best section. Downstream from Masemore Road to Falls Road would be my third choice.

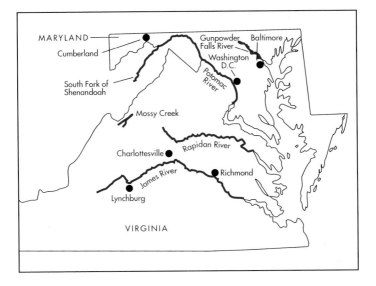

To reach the Gunpowder from Baltimore, take I-83 North to the Hereford exit. If you go west from this exit about one mile on Mt. Carmel Road, you'll come to Masemore Road on your right. The second road off Mt. Carmel, on the right, is Falls Road; turn onto it and in less than two miles you will reach the river below the dam.

To fish the stream from York Road, take a right (or go east) at the Hereford exit off I-83 and go one-quarter mile to Hereford, turn left (or north) and travel about two minutes on York Road to the bridge spanning the river.

POTOMAC RIVER
Maryland, Virginia, and District of Columbia

As it flows through western Maryland and Virginia down to the District of Columbia, the Potomac has long been considered one of the finest stretches of smallmouth bass water in the United States.

The Potomac is rugged and healthy, a freshwater ecosystem marked by nutrient-rich water and thriving populations of both baitfish and gamefish, of which the smallmouth bass is by far the most outstanding.

Considering the condition of the river only decades ago, struggling to survive, clogged as it was with algae as well as the onslaught of industrial and agricultural pollution, the comeback of the Potomac stands as one of the most remarkable river recovery stories in recent years. Indeed, the clean-up of the Potomac ranks as one of the nation's most outstanding environmental success stories.

Smallmouth bass fishing on the Potomac comes into its own in the spring and usually remains productive and active through the summer months and into the fall. The fishing is especially thrilling come the cool days and nights of late September and early October. As the air cools, so does the river, and the cooler water tends to make the bass more active than in the sluggish heat of the late summer months. As summer eases into fall, the river's smallmouth bass begin to change their feeding habits and tend to concentrate on minnows, which are in abundance in the river come autumn, moving along the river's weedy shoreline in thick schools.

Once the bass are set on minnows, a popping bug becomes one of the most effective flies. Potomac smallmouth bass, which can run to 18 inches or better, like to feed in the river's considerable current and eddies, so that whatever popper pattern is used, it should be kept moving, especially if you are trying to imitate the action of a swift-moving minnow.

A wide variety of popping bugs are popular and successful on the Potomac. One of the local favorites is the reliable

Potomac River Popper (#4 to #6), often called Lefty's Bug, which is simple, unpretentious, and quite deadly. The best colors for this pattern seem to be yellow, black, red, and white. Other productive favorites include Half & Halfs, Woolly Buggers, Dahlberg Divers, Clouser Deep Minnows, Muddler Minnows, Marabou Muddlers, Clouser Crayfish, marabou streamers and various hellgrammite patterns.

When fishing the Potomac in the fall, some of the most productive places along the river for smallmouth bass are the weedbeds along the banks of the river. These beds, which attract schooling minnows, likewise tend to attract feeding bass. The river's extensive rock gardens also provide current breaks and excellent cover for both bass and minnows and tend to hold great numbers of both.

Upper sections of the river, through Virginia and into northeastern West Virginia, offer some fine smallmouth bass fishing, with excellent bass habitat — swift, shallow water, rocky ledges, weedbeds, shoals, and pools. The bottom is fished more heavily on these sections of the river, in its deeper water or deep pools where a sinking line is required. When fishing streamers for smallmouth bass, it is usually best to cast across and downstream, followed by upstream and downstream mending to keep the fly working effectively.

The waters of the upper Potomac are now nutrient rich and support a wide diversity of aquatic insects, including mayflies. Locally, the most important of these, the White Miller, begins to come off the water at the end of July and will continue to hatch into August. White Millers emerge at dusk. Often there are dense clouds of them just above the surface of the water. Their life span is a matter of hours, during which time they emerge, mate, lay their eggs, and die. White Millers are a particular favorite among both the river's smallmouth bass and panfish populations, and the fish hit good imitations quite well, from nymphs to adult emergers.

The flow of the Potomac can change drastically from season to season, and from weather front to weather front. Generally, however, in the fall the river runs clear and shallow, which makes it a wonderful wading river. But getting the most out of the river in the fall usually means floating at least some of its sections. Indeed, a float trip on the Potomac is a super way of truly sampling the river's incredible smallmouth fishing. A number of local guides offer these trips.

Some of the more popular angling float trips are from the Chesapeake & Ohio Canal Lock #56 to Hancock, Maryland, which covers more than 10 miles of river; the Dam #4 to Snyders Landing — which covers less than eight miles of water — but every mile of it is first-class smallmouth water; and the Brunswick, Maryland to Route 15 Bridge run (close to Point of Rocks, Maryland, near the Virginia state line). Indeed, this lower section of the Potomac is considered by many fly fishermen to be some of the best smallmouth bass water in the country, marked all along its route by weedy edges, rocky shoals, and countless ledges, with bass hanging everywhere. Come spring, during the warming months of April and May, just before the bass spawn, this is superb smallmouth water, as spawning normally sends the fish into a prolonged feeding frenzy. Never are the smallmouths more active, more challenging, or present in greater numbers.

Throughout the summer, water levels in the river continue to drop and the current noticeably slows. More and more submerged grassbeds are revealed. By mid-summer the water has cleared considerably, and larger smallmouth bass begin congregating in the deeper water.

The summer is a great time to spend the day on the Potomac River catching plenty of smallmouth bass and panfish. Daily catches of up to a dozen nice fish are certainly not uncommon. And remember that as the days get hotter, the best time of day to fish is in the cooler mornings and late afternoons.

Further downstream, access is easy, at least from the Maryland side of the river, since most of the land along this section of the Potomac is part of the Chesapeake & Ohio Canal National Historic Park, which maintains more than a dozen boat launching sites.

There is excellent smallmouth fishing within only a few miles of the White House, just above Chain Bridge. The closest access to this fishing from Washington, D.C. is on the Virginia shore at Turkey Run Park. Access from the Maryland shore begins at Lock #6 of the C & O Canal, as well as Locks #8 and #10. These points are all within the Washington Beltway system.

Below Chain Bridge, which links Virginia to the District of Columbia, is the tidal basin of the river. For years, these waters were all but ignored because of pollution. Meanwhile, even though there are no smallmouths in this tidal water, the Potomac's tidal basin has developed into a thriving largemouth and striped bass fishery. It is clogged with grassbeds, both in the main channel and in the many feeder creeks and streams, as well as a great many sunken and abandoned wood structures, such as barges and docks, which provide an excellent largemouth bass habitat.

SOUTH FORK OF THE SHENANDOAH RIVER
Virginia

Not far from the upper reaches of the Potomac is another smallmouth bass river highly regarded by a great many fly fishermen, the South Fork of the beautiful Shenandoah

River, located south of Front Royal, Virginia. The South Fork is a rich limestone river, with a great swarm of bait-fish and other aquatic life, especially insects, all of which the smallmouths gorge on. Rather than flowing south, as most eastern rivers do, the Shenandoah flows to the north and east through the eastern tip of West Virginia and on through the great Shenandoah Valley of northern Virginia. The river's South Fork runs from down the eastern flank of the Massanutten Mountains. The North and South Forks join near Front Royal, Virginia, forming the river's main channel, which empties into the Potomac at Harper's Ferry, Virginia.

Smallmouth bass were introduced into the river in the mid-1800s, and within just a handful of years the South Fork of the river had already earned a reputation as one of the country's great smallmouth bass rivers. Despite a bleak period (as on the Potomac) of unregulated pollution, the South Fork has made a dramatic recovery and is again an outstanding bass river. On a good day, it is not unusual for a couple of lucky fly fishermen to hook as many as 100 smallies.

Management trial and error along the North Fork, South Fork, and main channel of the Shenandoah have, over the years, served to alter the size of the fish, but smallmouths on the South Fork can easily average 8 to 12 inches, and occasionally a bigger fish can be taken.

As on the upper Potomac, poppers (#4 to #8) work well on the South Fork as do Muddler Minnows, hair bugs, sculpin and leech imitations, as well as Matuka and Zonker streamers.

The South Fork is a great river to fish by jonboat, canoe, or rubber raft. Several excellent angling float trips on the Shenandoah are available out of Luray, Virginia. There are also many good areas for wading.

RAPIDAN RIVER AND MOSSY CREEK
Virginia

Beauty comes in many guises, takes many shapes and forms, nuances, and, perhaps, nowhere is the notion of natural beauty more exuberant, excessive, and diverse than the Blue Ridge Mountains and Great Smoky Mountains. These mountain ranges are laced with hundreds of productive and challenging trout and smallmouth bass rivers, creeks, and streams. Two are special favorites of mine, the Rapidan River and Mossy Creek.

Rapidan River

The upper reaches of the Rapidan River, as well as numerous catch-and-release streams in the vast Shenandoah National Park, offer fly fishermen memorable trout fishing, particularly for stocked and wild brook trout.

The Rapidan comes down fast out of the Blue Ridge, its channel cutting down between Madison and Culpeper, Virginia. Formed of many small feeder creeks, streams, and springs, the river takes on volume and size and character around Camp Hoover, where President Herbert Hoover often escaped from the stress and strain of political life to fish. Here the river is joined by the cold, fast waters of Laurel Fork and Mill Prong.

While Rapidan trout are plentiful, they are small — a big Rapidan brookie rarely goes beyond 12 inches. Even so, they are stunning fish, marked by beautiful ivory-edged fins. Fishing the Rapidan also puts the fly fisherman among some native brook trout in the rugged waters of the Staunton River, a tributary that joins the Rapidan within the boundaries of the Shenandoah National Park.

While Rapidan brook trout will remain active throughout most of the year, the spring and fall are the best times for fast action. The best patterns for these Rapidan brook trout are Mr. Rapidan Dry Fly (#14 to #18), Mr. Rapidan Emerger (#10 to #14), Shenk's Sulphur Dry (#16 to #18), and the March Brown (#12 to #14).

The river is accessible from any number of trails and old logging roads, and from the lodge at Big Meadows. For more information on the trails and roads that provide access to the Rapidan, as well as another 20 or so rivers in the Shenandoah National Park, Harry Murray has a good guidebook (see Appendix for his address).

Given its proximity to such large cities as Richmond, Washington, and Baltimore, there are times when the Rapidan and its sister mountain waters can be overcome with crowds. But such days are few, and there is so much solitude to the mountains that the determined angler can always find an unoccupied stretch of water.

The Rapidan and the Staunton are heavily restricted, that is, they can be fished only with barbless hooks and with artificial lures on a strictly catch-and-release basis. These rules hardly seem too contrary, though, considering the beauty of the river and the mountains. The trout are gladly released and more than one fly fisherman has fished these mountains trying to figure out a way of never having to leave them, of releasing himself with the trout. It is an angling experience that any fly fisherman would delight in.

Mossy Creek

Many of the fly fishermen who regularly fish Virginia's streams believe that the best of them all is Mossy Creek, a limestone spring creek closer in character to the trout streams of Pennsylvania than to the typical Blue Ridge trout stream. Mossy Creek (located near Harrisonburg, Virginia, northwest of Charlottesville) is surely one of the best brown trout streams south of Pennsylvania.

About three miles of the creek — which is the only area open to fishing — is protected by strict fishing rules and regulations. Each angler is required by law to have a special permit to fish this water, but they are available and free at local fly shops.

Mossy Creek can be fished successfully year-round. There are hatches along Mossy Creek, but they are closer, in nature, to those of spring creeks than to the hatches common on other Blue Ridge streams, with little, if any, mayfly activity. However, during the prime hatch seasons of the summer, standard dry patterns such as Adams, Light Cahill, and Tricos can be effective. Come autumn, Murray's Strymphs, as well as an assortment of nymph, sculpin, and hopper patterns, will generally get the attention of the feeding browns. During the spring and summer months, often the best offerings for Mossy Creek trout are terrestrials, especially beetles, ants, and hoppers.

The fishing on Mossy Creek is challenging, even difficult. But for those who are patient, there are hefty four to five-pound browns to be taken.

JAMES RIVER
Virginia

Of all the east coast's big smallmouth rivers, for a great many smallmouth fly fishermen, the best place for catching a trophy is Virginia's James River. What makes the James such an important and wonderful smallmouth bass river is that it is among only a small handful of smallmouth rivers in the Northeast and Middle Atlantic where the smallmouth fishery is actually improving, thriving, rather than declining and giving in to ever greater degrees of habitat destruction and pollution. But not the James.

Today, it produces not only far more smallmouth bass than at any other time during its history, it is also producing more and more big bass (four pounds and over). Only Virginia's Smith River rivals it for huge smallmouths, though the Smith does not seem to produce as many fish weighing over four pounds as does the James.

And these days, though it is still rare, fortunate fly fishermen are from time to time taking truly grand smallmouths from the James, five and six-pounders. The size of the James' bass is, however, less impressive than the staggering population of fish in the river. Good days on the James River are truly memorable days, haunting days, days full of bronzebacks, with catches easily reaching 50 to 100 fish a day.

In a state laced by fine rivers, the James is Virginia's biggest and longest and (many anglers believe) its loveliest. The headwaters of the James are found up in the wild, hard-edged country of the Allegheny Mountains, then as the river runs southeast, rising and falling through the mountains and piedmont country, it coils on toward Richmond and then on to its eventual union with the salty waters of the Chesapeake Bay.

The James is a superb smallmouth river throughout most of its watershed above Richmond. From below the city to down where it empties into the Chesapeake Bay, smallmouth bass fishing also gives way to occasional excellent runs of largemouth bass and shad. But it is for the river's fabled bronzebacks that fly fishermen fall under the James' spell.

Although large crowds do descend on the James — particularly on the Lynchburg section of the river — there is so much river to fish that there is no reason why any angler should have to fight the crowds. Because if it's shoulder to shoulder above and below Lynchburg, there is always quiet, unoccupied water near Big Island, Bremo Bluff, Glasgow, Cartersville, or Buchanan.

Most sections of the river can be fished by boat or canoe, or by wading. Naturally, floating the river will give you a chance to fish more of the river and experience more of its beauty and its fish. Although there are several rough spots along the James (detailed maps are essential for any angler planning to float the river alone, without a guide), for the most part the river is one of the great canoeing rivers of the East, and there are few greater angling pleasures than lazily canoeing the river, fly fishing for its bass as you go.

Wading and bank fishing along the James can also produce exciting fishing and amazing days. If a wading angler cannot cover as much water as a fisherman in a boat, he can usually cover it better, getting his line over every bit of water that looks like it might hold fish.

Early summer, beginning in late June, through early autumn, usually mid-October, is the best time to fly fish the James. During these months, the water is rich in food and it is warm.

Despite their number and size, James River smallmouth do not really require any special gear, flies, or fishing techniques. A good bass rod, with say, a 7 to 9-weight line (an 8-weight is probably the best), and a vest full of a variety of standard bass poppers and streamers (#2 to #6) and a few large nymphs (any of the flies mentioned for use on the Potomac are perfectly suitable) will give any fly fisherman a chance to experience the exceptional wonders of the James and its smallmouth bass.

OVERLEAF: *The flats off the Florida Keys are a fly-fishing paradise for the saltwater angler.*

CHAPTER THREE

THE SOUTH
AND MIDWEST

LAKE OKEECHOBEE
Florida

In addition to the unmatched splendor of the Florida Keys and Biscayne Bay, of the backcountry of the mighty Everglades, its west coast — including the Ten Thousand Islands area — and its more than 400 miles of coastline, the state of Florida also has more than 58,000 square miles of freshwater rivers and lakes.

Indeed, Florida's unique and diverse array of saltwater and freshwater fishing habitats clearly makes it a state that can truly claim to be an angler's paradise. What it lacks in natural beauty it more than makes up for in miles and miles of water, seemingly endless numbers and species of gamefish and year-round fishing.

If tarpon and snook, bonefish and permit anglers crowd into Florida each year so, too, do thousands and thousands of dedicated bass anglers, including fly fishermen who delight in taking the state's famous populations of largemouth bass on the fly rod.

The Florida largemouth bass is a distinct subspecies known most of all for its size. These bass are perhaps the biggest (or at least consistently so) in the country. And nowhere in Florida do they get any bigger than in the vast sprawl of Lake Okeechobee, where eight to 10-pound largemouth bass can often be as common as the five-pounders.

The lake, which covers more than 700 miles (or 450,000 acres) is considered to be one of the premier largemouth bass lakes in the nation. Its shallow, warm, rich waters allow the bass to grow and remain active year-round. Because they enjoy a 12-month growth cycle, Okeechobee bass are big, even for Florida bass. Because the lake averages only 10 to 12 feet in depth, it has great stands of reeds, pepper grass, and bulrushes which provide excellent cover for bass and the baitfish they feed on.

The best fishing usually occurs in shallow water — between six and eight feet deep — in which the bass are tempted to strike at the surface or at shallow-running patterns, which allows the fly fisherman to use a greater assortment of flies.

Even though Lake Okeechobee is one of the largest freshwater lakes in the country, and even though it is located in the midst of Florida's seemingly endless growth, it is, as yet, not pressed by any major centers of population. (The nearest towns are Okeechobee, Clewiston, Moore Haven, and Belle Glade, while the nearest large city is Palm Beach, 65 miles away from the little town of Okeechobee.) And because of the lake's size, crowds — even the very few times when there are crowds — never seem like crowds. There is always isolated water to be found somewhere on the lake.

Some bass fishermen stay away from Okeechobee because they claim that it does not produce truly heavy largemouth bass with the consistency of some of the other noted Florida bass lakes, such as Rodman's Reservoir. But while the lake may not be full of 15-pounders, its waters

FLORIDA

Ft. Pierce

Lake
Okeechobee

Naples

Ten Thousand Islands

Miami

Key West

Florida Keys

do seem to produce an endless stream of sizeable bass, and the chance of that lunker is always there.

While the bass fishing on the lake is productive all year long, serious bass fishermen like to fish the lake from February through April, when the bass tend to be in the shallows and in the grassbeds. During the spring, it is not unusual for fly fishermen to take from 10 to 20 bass a day weighing two pounds and up. (If you plan on keeping fish, the limit is 10 bass a day per angler.)

Okeechobee bass hit a great variety of popping bugs, including White Peck's Poppers as well as Green Gaines Minnow Poppers. Larger streamers, equipped with weed-guards, are effective, too. A floating line is all that's needed since the lake is so shallow.

This unbelievable bass fishing extends beyond the lake into the nearby marshes of the Everglades backcountry east of Okeechobee in Palm Beach county, which consists of a sea of grass spreading from the lake into numerous channels, dikes, and ditches, all of which hold bass. While the spring may be the best time for bass on the lake itself, the fall is certainly the best time to try for the bass in this backcountry water, where the bass hold in the deep pools and ditches as the shallow pools and ponds begin to dry up. During such times a neatly cast popping bug stands a good chance of bringing a strike.

A word of caution, especially about these backcountry, Everglades bass. They have been found in recent years to carry high levels of mercury in their flesh. Eating them is not recommended. So most fly fishermen fish this area strictly as a catch-and-release sport.

TEN THOUSAND ISLANDS
Florida

For many anglers who have moved from the north to southern Florida, the place that is the most fun to fish is not the fabled Florida Keys. Instead, it is the Ten Thousand Islands region. In fact, many of these anglers have never visited the Keys, because the Ten Thousand Islands area contains everything they want in a fly-fishing paradise.

The domain of the Ten Thousand Islands runs roughly from just south of Naples on Florida's west coast to near

Homestead and upper Key Largo. Almost all of it lies totally within the Everglades National Park. It is a unique natural area. There is really no place in the United States exactly like it.

Freshwater that slowly spreads down on the sheet of limestone coral that forms the base for the Everglades seeps into the part of Florida bordering huge Florida Bay, one of the saltiest bodies of water in the country. As a result, the Ten Thousand Islands (and nobody has ever counted them as far as I know, but there are probably many more than that) is surrounded by a mix of fresh, brackish, and in some cases, pure saltwater.

The area has been best described as a fish factory. Its waters are incredibly fertile. There are large open coves and sounds, such as Tarpon Bay; or Whitewater Bay, an aptly named place, where the wind can turn the water into froth as waves beat against each other; as well as innumerable small mangrove islands. Deep rivers also penetrate the area, some reaching inland so far that their upper borders end in the Everglades where their shorelines become lined with sawgrass instead of mangrove trees. In such a diverse habitat, some of it rarely penetrated by man, all sorts of aquatic creatures can spawn and flourish.

The shrimp that is so common to the Florida Keys is known to migrate more than one hundred miles from the Dry Tortugas, west of Key West, to spawn in these rich waters. Snook, snapper, huge jewfish, redfish, freshwater drum, tarpon, and a host of other species all use the Ten Thousand Islands as a nursery ground. Many species are lifelong residents of these creeks and bays.

The Islands are composed primarily of red mangrove trees, and all the creeks and rivers that feed freshwater into the area from the Everglades are lined with them. The root system of these mangrove trees, deeply buried in the rocky coral, is able to resist hurricanes and stand firm against anything nature can throw at the region. In fact, skippers often take their boats into mangrove creeks during hurricanes because they offer safe haven. These mangrove root systems also provide a refuge for small baitfish, crabs, oysters and other foods that predator fish feed upon, sometimes from ambush holds among the roots.

If you have not spent considerable time fishing the Ten Thousand Islands, *do not attempt to fish the area without a guide, as it is very easy to become lost* among these islands that, to the uninitiated, all look the same.

But successful fishing here is more than just knowing how to get around and get home safely. You need to understand the movement of the surface and subsurface water that slowly seeps down from the Everglades, and its effect upon the feeding patterns of the various sport species. You need also to understand how cold and hot weather affect the movements of the fish. And near Florida Bay, where the waters of the creeks and bays are affected by tidal action, you need to have a knowledge of local tides, which, of course, exert a substantial influence upon the feeding behavior of gamefish. So for safety and fishing success in these waters, an experienced guide or a friend with good local knowledge is vital.

The Ten Thousand Islands area is principally a shallow watershed; only its rivers and some of its creeks contain deep water. Therefore, a fly rod and a floating line are good tools for fishing here. The crashing of a plug or jig onto the surface often frightens fish. In fact, in many situations, fly tackle is by far the best tackle that can be used. For example, when tarpon, snook or redfish are cruising the shoreline, or moving across open, shallow bays, the delicate presentation that is only possible with a fly is going to be the most productive presentation. And no tackle is as accurate and effective as fly tackle when casting to a mangrove shoreline that may hold snook or redfish hiding in an ambush position under the roots. With the use of a weedless Lefty's Deceiver or a Clouser Deep Minnow, equipped with a weedguard, or a bend-back-style streamer fly, you can fish with little fear of snagging in the root system of the mangroves, and the ability to drop the fly softly in front of a fish, and then retrieve it slowly, can be a devastating technique to score on tarpon, snook and redfish.

Fishing is good in the Ten Thousand Islands from the northern edge of the area around Marco Island (near Naples, Florida) through all the water to the southern end at Whitewater Bay. It should be noted that guides can only be booked at the northern and southern ends of the region — the rest of it is uninhabited. And, except for during those uncommon periods of extreme cold fronts, fishing can be good all year long.

The small community of Flamingo is a jumping-off point for fishing the southern (or lower) and mid-section of the region. However, at this writing the fishing in Florida Bay near Flamingo is being devastated by an alga that biologists are trying to understand in order, hopefully, to eliminate it in the future. However, the land mass that separates Florida Bay from the Ten Thousand Islands has thus far not been affected by this algae plague.

At the northern extremity of the area, anglers can book guides from Naples or Marco Island that employ flats boats to penetrate this wonderful wilderness. One of the best of the Naples area guides is Captain Jim Grace, with whom I have spent many fine days fishing this region.

In recent years, strict laws have been enacted regulating the harvest of snook and redfish. This has served to increase fish populations, so that today, Ten Thousand

Islands probably represents the best place in the country to seek both of these species — especially with a fly rod.

If I had to choose one place in southern Florida (including even the Keys) where I could have the most saltwater fun with a light fly rod (an 8-weight is ideal) I would immediately select the Ten Thousand Islands.

FLORIDA KEYS
Florida

During the last decade, saltwater fly fishing has enjoyed a dramatic increase in popularity, particularly in the pursuit of bonefish, tarpon, and permit.

Today the fly fisherman is faced with the most difficult of decisions — whether to make his usual spring migration to one of the country's premier trout rivers, or undertake a journey south, south to the warm Caribbean flats of the Florida Keys, where some of the best fishing occurs in mid-to-late spring, particularly for the tarpon who are typically beginning to move into the Florida Keys as early summer takes hold.

Also, many American fly fishermen are beginning to divide their angling year into fresh and saltwater seasons, giving trout their complete attention from April until the big brown trout runs of the fall, and then heading south for the Keys, where the best bonefishing month of all may be October and where, even in the winter months, there are still plenty of tarpon and permit.

No matter what a fly fisherman's saltwater destination, perhaps his most important consideration in planning for angling success is not so much his own skill, experience, or equipment. But rather, the key to success in saltwater flats fishing, the essential requirement above all else, as far as I'm concerned — especially in the crowded and competitive waters of the Florida Keys — is the selection of a good guide: a guide who knows the water and how each species reacts to changes in water conditions and temperature; a guide who is an expert at finding and spotting elusive bonefish and permit and tarpon; a guide who not only knows how to fish for these species but who can easily transfer his knowledge to his client. Finding a good guide takes an investment of time and effort. But it is an investment that will pay remarkable dividends, both in terms of good fishing and an enjoyable fishing trip.

In the Florida Keys, many of the best saltwater guides are booked a year in advance, so it is always best to start looking for a guide at least a year ahead of your trip. Typically, the best guides are those whose names are passed around by word of mouth.

Serious saltwater fly fishermen travel the globe, but invariably they find their way back to the Florida Keys, where the flats offer not only some of the most exciting and challenging saltwater fly fishing in the world, but a stunning choice of guides, excellent, reliable boats, all fully loaded with a vast array of tackle and rods, and many other amenities not so easily found in most third world saltwater fly-fishing destinations. On shore, of course, the Keys offer the angler everything from endlessly tempting tackle shops to too many good restaurants offering too much wonderful seafood.

Wherever you decide to fish throughout the Florida Keys and Biscayne Bay, the number and variety of locally tied flies for bonefish and permit and tarpon are truly astounding and ever changing. For bonefish and permit, the patterns of choice are nearly always some imitation of

OVERLEAF: *Angler casting off the coast of the Florida Keys.*

shrimp and crab. The vast selection of colorful tarpon flies is much more intimidating.

While there are trusted traditional flies for each species, selecting saltwater flies to fish the Keys is perhaps best done in the Keys, in close cooperation with guides, who should know what is best for the current water and weather conditions, what the fish are most likely to hit, and so on.

While the Florida Keys are often spoken and written of as though they were a single place, they are, in fact, a handsome strand or archipelago of islands scattered like jewels over 150 miles of the warm blue Atlantic from Key Biscayne to the Dry Tortugas. Many anglers do not consider themselves properly in the Keys until they are safely in Key Largo, south of Miami.

If you count any island, regardless of size, as a key, then the chain includes as least a thousand islands. If you count only the larger islands, then the number shrinks to two or three hundred. Twenty-five of these keys are bound together by the Florida Overseas Highway that ends at Key West.

The Keys were first opened up to the outside world (and to many curious anglers) beginning in 1912 when Henry Flagler's railroad began carrying tourists there.

While the Keys are a coherent group of islands, they share different geological origins. As you travel south and then west from Key Biscayne down to Marathon, to your right is Florida Bay, which has geological origins similar to those of the Appalachian Mountains, with a bottom of soft silt and no coral. On your left is the Atlantic Ocean, with a bottom structure that has developed on the remains of old coral reefs. These differing geological structures provide a wide diversity of shallow water conditions that attract and hold a great many different species of fish.

Fishing is excellent throughout the Keys, from Biscayne Bay, to Jewfish Key near Key Largo, down through Tavernier, Bahia Honda Key, Big Pine Key, Cudjoe Key, Key West, and on to the Marquesas and the Dry Tortugas. The tapestry of shallow flats, keys, backcountry, lakes, and channels that makes up the Keys covers more than 4,000 square miles of saltwater shallows. The waters of the Keys are tropical and consequently attract a full complement of tropical species. Besides bonefish and tarpon, fly fishermen come principally for permit, barracuda, shark, snapper, redfish, and snook.

At the upper end of the Keys, shimmering beyond the neon reflections of the Miami skyline, is the deep, turquoise beauty of Biscayne Bay, which may offer, in my view, the best bonefish water in south Florida, including the Keys. Down below Fisher Island and Virginia Key, on the Biscayne Flats near Soldier Key, are where Florida's wary, elusive big bonefish run. These near perfect saltwater flats begin near Rickenbacker Causeway and run all the way down to Key Largo. Bonefish on these Biscayne flats typically go four to six pounds and there have been fish taken there weighing over 12 pounds. The best time for these Biscayne bonefish is in April and May.

Often the best fishing is south of Soldier Key, around the Ragged Keys, Sands Key, and Elliot Key, with bonefish and permit found on both the bay and ocean side of these islands. The bonefish and permit fishing along the famous Featherbed Bank of Biscayne Bay usually holds up from spring through the fall. Indeed, there is first-class, quality fishing in the bay all year-round. And Biscayne Bay should not be overlooked when it comes for a chance to take big tarpon. For example, often larger tarpon (up to l00 pounds) are found in what is called Government Cut, which is the ship channel into the port of Miami.

One of the most popular spots for fly fishermen has become Islamorada, located between Upper and Lower Matecumbe Key. Islamorada may very well be the best known of the country's saltwater destinations, since it has received a great amount of publicity from the articles which regularly appear in the fly-fishing press, as well as from the general press, which has gone there to cover the fishing trips of such celebrities as George Bush, our former President (regrettably, not a fly fisherman).

Islamorada's legendary guides and its legendary bonefish and tarpon populations have both become ever more popular, so that angling crowds are quickly becoming a problem, especially for the saltwater fly fisherman who is searching for a degree of solitude in which to pursue bonefish, permit and tarpon. But, the water off Islamorada holds a great many fish, particularly along Long Key and Buchanan Bank, where the fish are active beginning in late spring and throughout the summer. Tarpon usually show up in March and will be around in the early part of the summer. Some big bonefish are always in this area.

While the flats off the Keys (and in Biscayne Bay) are not known for their great populations of bonefish, they are known for their big bonefish, some going as large as 12 pounds or heavier.

Marathon, which is halfway between Islamorada and Key West, offers some incredible flats fishing, as well. There are almost as many guides here as in Islamorada, and the extensive chain of mangrove keys in this area holds a surprising number of gamefish, not only tarpon and bonefish, but permit as well. Anglers who fish Marathon often tell tales of taking all these species in a single day's fishing (the saltwater "grand slam").

The fishing off Key West is almost as good, so good sometimes, that its flats are crowded with guides and clients who have commuted from Marathon and Isla-morada. Without question, the best chances for big flats permit in the Keys are probably off Key West, east to Big Pine Key, and west to the Marquesas, an isolated group of islands near Key West that is also celebrated for its large tarpon population.

And besides, at Key West, after the fishing, there are a number of watering holes such as Sloppy Joe's or the Half-Shell Raw Bar, all of which provide the necessary atmosphere and ingredients for transferring the wonder of fishing the flats deep into the folds of memory.

WHITE AND NORFORK RIVERS
Arkansas

Looking north from Sherman Mountain, in northwest Arkansas, the highest peak of the Ozark Mountains (2,280 feet), the rounded, eroded peaks of the Ozark range look like a shattered dinosaurian backbone. Geo-logically, the Ozarks are young mountains indeed, dating back perhaps 450 million years. Actually, the entire Ozark plateau is the remnant of an ancient sea floor that passing time and erosion have sculpted into low-slung, hog-back mountains separating the drainages of the Missouri and Arkansas rivers.

The Ozarks are one of the planet's great aquifers. Throughout these mountains of shale and sandstone, limestone and dolomite, are numerous great sinks and springs and rushing underground rivers. The region has more freshwater springs than any other region of the country except Florida, cold springs like Mammoth Springs, Greer Springs, and Big Springs, the latter of which alone, moves a billion gallons of water a day.

Because of this system of sinks and springs and underground rivers, the Ozark Mountains are the watershed for many rivers and lakes, creeks and streams throughout Missouri and Arkansas, including the Current River, the Little Red, the Strawberry, the Norfork, and the White.

The White River and its sister river, the Norfork, are located in the high country of central Arkansas, near the Missouri border, falling out of the massive Bull Shoals Lake and Lake Norfork in Marion and Baxter counties, between Flippin and Mountain Home. The White is in hardluck mountain country, a land still edged with wildness, mountains of deep, rugged beauty, the river falling from the Bull Shoals Lake south to Buffalo City, where it is joined by the wild water of the Buffalo River, and where it then bends back to the north and east to Norfork and its juncture with the Norfork River, before falling again to the south and its union with the Arkansas River.

Before federal dam projects at Bull Shoals and Greers Ferry and Norfork were undertaken and completed in the early 1950s, the rivers of the region — the White, the Buffalo, the Little Red, and so on — were warm-water bass rivers, home to the cunning and fierce Arkansas smallmouth. Indeed, the area still offers some smallmouth fishing on Crooked Creek, Mill Creek, the South Fork, and the deeply beautiful Piney Creek. You can also continue to find huge numbers of largemouth bass, spotted bass, white bass, and panfish on the Norfork and Bull Shoals lakes. And Lake Norfork is considered to be one of the country's best striped bass watersheds.

Construction of the dams, especially those at Bull Shoals and Norfork, completely changed the nature and character of the rivers. The White, which had been a warm-water river, became a cold-water river, with an average year-round water temperature of 55 degrees. Bass

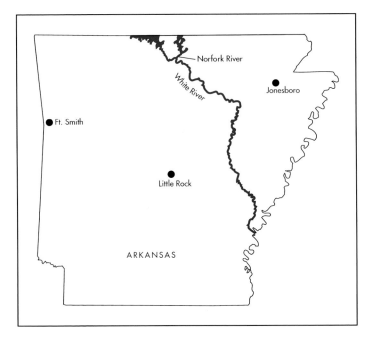

water became nearly perfect trout water: fast, cold, clean, rich in crustaceans — shrimp, scuds, sowbugs — baitfish, and insects, aquatic and terrestrial.

Almost immediately, the state of Arkansas undertook a program of stocking the White and the Norfork rivers with trout, and within a decade, so successful was the program that both rivers had earned a reputation of being perhaps the South's finest trout waters.

The White's cold waters make it an excellent year-round trout river. Because of the dams, the manipulation of the river and its flow, the stocked trout, especially the rainbows, rarely reproduce naturally in the river. Even so, for stocked trout, those on the White grow rapidly, and the stocked browns (but not generally the rainbows) are often as fierce and difficult as wild fish.

Indeed, the White has become one of the great brown trout rivers in the country, luring anglers from around the world eager to have a go at one of the river's brown behemoths. Although not by any means routinely caught on fly tackle, the river holds a meaningful population of record-sized browns, brooding, moody, difficult trout that can be as large as 15 to 20 pounds, and even more. Therein lies the river's unique fly-fishing challenge!

The mood of these rivers is to a large extent dictated by the dams, by how many generators are running at any given time. The changing water flow and volume has a great deal to do with the quality of fishing.

When the water drops, the White takes on an almost tranquil nature. Down on the lower stretches of the river, the water is shallow enough for wading the big, trout-filled blue-green pools and shoals of faster water splashing over beds of smooth stones.

When the water is up, the river seems almost western in temper — big, broad, powerful. Anglers move up and down the river in jonboats, working the edges of the swift current. The iridescent flanks of the rainbow and cut-throat trout flash in the translucent water.

Although many species of fish have been released in these cold-water Arkansas rivers. So far, it is the browns and rainbows and cutthroats that have dominated, survived, thrived. The rainbows in the White are on the average not as large as the browns, generally running from 10 to 16 inches. But a good day on the White River or Norfork can be an incredible day, with anglers catching and releasing more than 100 trout before sunset. Patience and a good guide are the keys to fly fishing these rivers. *Your guide's local knowledge of the dams' generating schedules and resultant water levels and flow on the rivers will be an essential key to your fly-fishing success.* And while there are hundreds, even thousands, of guides plying these rivers, most cater to bait fishermen, and regrettably, pay little or no attention to high-water problems, fish kills, water pollution, and the other environmental matters that are important to the fly fisherman. *There are only a handful or so of dedicated professional fly-fishing guides working on the White and Norfork waters, so the successful fly fisherman will be the prudent one who has gone out of his way to find and hire one.* A good way to do this is to deal through a reputable fly-fishing shop in the area.

While the big dams have changed the nature of the White and the Norfork, turned them from warm-water bass rivers to cold-water trout rivers, the change did not produce natural trout rivers. Because the dams are constantly either storing water or using water to generate electricity, the rivers do not have a truly natural life cycle of their own. While there are hatches on the White and Norfork rivers, these are not pristine dry-fly rivers, and the traditional dry-fly fisherman may be disappointed in the angling here.

While the White provides excellent fishing throughout the year, the best time for big trout is from late fall (November) through March, particularly during spawning time for the browns. The big browns are extremely difficult fish to catch, particularly with a fly, and often vex even the most accomplished fly fisherman. The best flies for this time of year include various sowbug (#14 to #18), shad (#4 to #6) and sculpin (#4 to #8) patterns, as well as Gold Matukas (#4 to #8), Muddler Minnows (#6 to #10), Olive Woolly Buggers (#8 to #10), Squirrel Nymphs (#12), Glo-Bugs (#10), Blue-Winged Olives (#18 to #20), and midges (#18 to #24).

The only significant dry-fly action on the White and Norfork occurs in the spring, and the best dry patterns for this activity include Light Cahills (#16), Sulphur Duns (#18), and Elk-Hair Caddis (#14 to #20). Other popular patterns for the spring include March Browns and Gold-Ribbed Hare's Ear Nymphs (#12 to #16), and caddis pupa (#14 to #16) and cranefly pupa (#8 to #10) imitations.

Most of the spring and winter patterns — streamers, nymphs and drys — will continue to perform well in the summer and fall on the White and Norfork. But during this time you should also include in your fly box a variety of hopper patterns (#8 to #10).

As with the brown trout, the rainbow and cutthroat trout on the White River are heavily fished. Consequently, fly selection and presentation are critical, as the bigger trout of all three species are finicky and especially spooky.

AU SABLE AND PERE MARQUETTE RIVERS
Michigan

Au Sable River

In the long and notable history of fly fishing in America, the legend and legacy of Michigan's magnificent Au Sable River is perhaps second only to New York's Beaverkill. Called La Belle Riviere aux Sables by early French trappers, the Au Sable was being hailed as the country's best trout fishery before the War Between the States.

Like the Beaverkill, the Au Sable's fame and its reputation among fly fishers have led to considerable crowding during weekends in May and June. Anglers wanting to experience the river and its trout on weekends during these months would be wise to schedule their fishing for the very early mornings or late evenings. These times are least used by other anglers and by the often abundant canoeists. After June, the number of weekend anglers and canoeists drops off sharply. Regardless of the month, weekdays are always less crowded than weekends.

The Au Sable rises in the high country of central Michigan and flows east and south through Michigan's lower peninsula on its way to Lake Huron. This is "Big Woods" country and the great river mirrors the uncommon beauty of this surrounding countryside.

The three branches of the Au Sable are named aptly enough, the North Branch, South Branch, and Main Stream. The headwaters of the North Branch are at Lake Otsego. From the lake downstream to the town of Lovells, the water is notable for its wonderful, native brook trout fishery. Note, however, that much of this area is privately owned and not readily accessible to the casual fly fisher.

The South Branch tumbles through isolated country near Roscommon. This is the wildest section on the entire river system and features the George Mason Memorial Tract, named in honor of the man who spent a large portion of his life and his fortune to ensure that the South Branch will endure, untouched by development.

The South Branch is dominated by wild browns, but big brookies can also be found sheltering in its cool waters. Special regulations assure a strong population of good-sized trout, and much of the water is readily accessible.

The Main Stream begins west of Grayling and flows through town. While it's quite fishable in these upper reaches, most anglers head downstream a few miles to the flies-only section between Burton's Landing and Wakeley Bridge. Often called the "Holy Water," this section is marked with "sweepers," downed trees whose branches drag in the currents. These tangles and knots of trees provide the trout with many places to hide and feed.

Because the currents of the Main Stream are quite strong, most anglers find it easiest to fish the sweepers by wading downstream. Such wading is delightful because, like the North and South Branches, the Main Stream has a fine gravel bottom with very few obstacles. In addition, by fishing down, the best holding lies can be reached by simply casting down and across the stream and mending according to the push or pull of the currents.

Below the Holy Water, the North Branch and then the South Branch join the Main Stream, swelling it to true river proportions. This section of the Main Stream has some fine fishing and is best reached by drifting.

Just upstream from the town of Mio (35 miles east of Grayling), Big Creek joins the Au Sable. From the town of Luzerne to the mouth, this trout stream offers several miles of fishable water where strong hatches can cause good surface feeding. In the heat of summer, anglers often fish the pool where the cool waters of Big Creek join with the tepid waters of the Main Stream.

Down to Mio, the trident Au Sable provides over 200 miles of trout stream. At Mio, a low-head, hydroelectric dam creates a modest lake. Locally know as "Mio Pond," this stillwater area holds some truly large trout. In addition to temporarily stilling the strong flows of the Au Sable, the Mio dam is a landmark that separates the free-flowing upper section of the Au Sable from the much-dammed, middle section.

Flowing through a series of six dams, the middle section consists of deep pools spaced by sweeping bends, where waters run smooth but swift. There are big trout here. In the past, large water releases from the dams caused quickly changing, often hazardous, conditions on this middle section, but under a new F.E.R.C. relicensing agreement, sudden, heavy releases have now ceased. However, it is still tough water to fish, due to its breadth and the sheer volume of its flow.

Like the middle section, the lower section of the river, from Foote Dam to the mouth, is big water. While there are some large resident browns here, this water is mostly a spawning area for Lake Huron steelhead, browns, and salmon. Eager fish can begin moving into the river as early as mid-August, but heavy runs really begin in September and continue through November. A second steelhead run occurs in March and April. Anglers searching for anadromous fisheries will like it here.

Without a doubt, the most famous hatch on the Au Sable is that of the Giant Michigan Mayfly or Hex (*Hexigena limbata*). It comes just at or after dark during the last half of June and gives the fly fisher the best chance of the year to take a big brown on a dry fly. Fishing the Au Sable in the black of night, blindly casting huge #2 and #4 imitations toward the crashing sounds of a big, feeding fish, and then feeling its surging take, is an experience long remembered.

But the quality of a fishery is not measured by one hatch. Rather, it is based on the quality of all its hatches. Beginning with the Hendrickson Mayfly and Popcorn Caddis in late April and early May, the river offers a full plate of hatches through the season. All the major and minor hatches can be experienced on the Au Sable. In addition to the two opening hatches, one can find Blue Quill, Light Hendrickson, Gray Drake, Brown Drake, Great Mahogany Dun, Trico, Blue-Winged Olive, and many other varieties of mayfly hatches, in addition to copious emergences of caddises, stoneflies, and midges. Often several species will be emerging and egg laying at the same time, giving the angler a severe test of his observational and diagnostic skills. It is the challenges, however, that have made this no ordinary river.

Pere Marquette River

Many fly fishermen believe Michigan's Pere Marquette River rivals the Au Sable as both a trout and steelhead river, with a recovering population of handsome brown and rainbow trout.

This river has been through good times and bad, and has only in recent years recovered its full vitality as a trout river. Nevertheless, its history as one of the country's premier trout rivers is long and deep. Some of the first brown trout eggs that arrived in the United States in the late 1880s were sent to the Pere Marquette and the river (along with New York's Beaverkill), quickly became one of the country's first notable brown trout rivers.

During the first half of this century, indiscriminate clear-cutting of the forests of the river valley nearly ruined the river. The native graylings disappeared, as did stocked brook trout and some stocked cutthroats. But the brown trout hung on, as have the river's salmon, which were introduced into the river in the 1960s. The King or chinook salmon is now the dominant salmon on the river.

The main stem of the Pere Marquette begins about a half-mile east of State Route 37 in Lake County. Anglers usually divide the Pere Marquette into four sections — the lower river, the middle river, the flies-only section of the river, and the river's tributaries, which include the Little South Branch and the Middle Branch. These sections, along with the Baldwin River, form the Pere Marquette. There are trout in Little South Branch and Middle Branch, as well as in the Baldwin River down below the dense Baldwin-Luther Swamp.

The flies-only section of the Pere Marquette runs eight miles from near the Forks to Gleason's Landing. From Gleason's Landing on toward Walhalla, the river widens and deepens, offering some of the river's best trout fishing, possibly because it is the hardest part of the river to fish.

There are still some classic Michigan hatches along the Pere Marquette, including Hendricksons and spinners in the spring. Indeed, in May, along some stretches of the river, it is possible to fish for both steelhead and trout. By early summer, it is time for the Black Caddis and Sulphurs, Gray Drakes, and clouds of spinners during the late afternoons and early evenings. In addition to hatch imitations, Woolly Buggers and Muddler Minnows work just as well on the river, too, as do a wide assortment of terrestrial patterns.

GANGLER'S NORTH SEAL RIVER LODGE

Manitoba

There are many reasons why I like to fish, especially fly fish, although I enjoy using all kinds of tackle. Here are just some of the reasons that get my blood pumping.

There is a special thrill when sneaking up on a tailing bonefish or redfish, which is as anxious as a cat in a dog pound. You know that if there is one small mistake the game is over. A similar experience is to carefully observe a large trout in slick water that is sipping something from the surface. Your mind races to figure out what fly will fool it and how you can make a presentation without spooking the trophy. Many people are turned on when they hook a tarpon and it explodes into the air with flapping gills. But for me, one of the most exciting moments is when a huge tarpon lazily rolls upward from the depths, opens that cavernous mouth, and sucks in a fly. All of this seems to occur in a slow, deliberate action that allows your mind to capture every moment. There are many other reasons I like fly fishing.

I caught my first northern pike in 1948 on Lake Baskatong, Quebec. I caught the pike, but that pike hooked me. When a pike takes a fly it doesn't mess around. It may slowly follow a retrieve or it may launch itself like a rocket. But once it decides it is going to strike, the huge, tooth-filled mouth opens and the fly disappears inside. No two pike are alike. One may fight you all the way to the boat, another, possibly bigger, may come in like a sullen child approaching a scolding mother. But once it gets near you, it seems to go crazy, thrashing and leaping from the water.

I admit that many fish fight better than northern pike. But with the exception of a teased billfish, I believe that no species offers more visual excitement just before and during the moment the pike takes the fly. Pike fishing often takes place in only 2–5 feet of water near the shoreline, where the water is filled with aquatic vegetation or lily pads. Smallmouth bass have short bodies and large tails to make sharp turns as they pursue their quarry. But barracuda, king mackerel, and northern pike have long, tapered bodies. They can't make a sharp turn when pursuing a baitfish. These long, slender species launch themselves like a rocket so that their prey doesn't have a chance to make an escape turn.

Quite often a pike will be just under the surface when it decides to capture a fly. When it launches itself, the pike's body creates a slight wake in the water that rolls toward the fly. And if the pike is moving through weeds or lily pads, the vegetation rocks back and forth as the pike speeds toward the fly. All of these signals of an impending strike make the northern pike one of my favorite species.

I've fished for northern pike in many places, but today if you want a true fly-fishing trophy approaching or surpassing 20 pounds, you need to go to the far north of Canada or parts of Alaska. There are a number of lodges in Saskatchewan and Manitoba that offer great pike fishing, and while I can recommend several from personal experience, my preference is Gangler's North Seal River Lodge in northern Manitoba. The Gangler family has a long history of operating some of the finest fishing lodges in remote northern Canada. The lodge is located in the extreme northwest corner of Manitoba — a true wilderness area visited by very few people.

Lefty with a fly-caught pike at North Seal River Lodge, Canada.

To get to Gangler's North Seal River Lodge you take a charter plane from Manitoba, which lands within easy walking distance of the lodge. And what a lodge! It is a huge wooden structure of more than 4,000 square feet that blends into the surrounding wilderness. Intrepid builders slowly hauled the lumber and other materials over the snowy landscape and frozen lakes in the dead of winter — a magnificent accomplishment in itself. It is a Five-Star lodge and the meals are as good as you would get in a fine restaurant. Guests stay in individual cabins.

When at Gangler's North Seal River lodge you will have the opportunity to catch northern pike, walleyes, lake trout, and arctic grayling at Lake Egenolf. For fly fishermen the best time to book the lodge is the last week of June and the first two weeks of July. At this time, unless there is a very unusual weather pattern, aggressive northern pike cruise the shallows in the hundreds of small bays. Many of these exceed 12 pounds, and there are enough 20-pounders lurking there to make life very interesting.

You can stay at the lodge and fish Lake Egenolf or you can fly out to more than thirty other lakes, always accompanied with a guide. Or you can spend the week at one of the large number of outpost camps, each located on a lake teeming with fish.

Fly fishermen will want an 8- or 9-weight rod for pike and walleyes and a light trout rod (4-, 5-, or 6-weight) for grayling. Most of the lake trout range from 5–10 pounds, but some are up to 30 pounds, and for these you should have a 9- or 10-weight rod.

In my fifty years of northern pike fishing, I have never needed the huge flies that many experts recommend. Instead, I've caught many pike weighing 20 pounds or more on the Half & Half, Lefty's Deceiver, and Whistler on size

1/0 or 2/0 hooks. These should be no longer than 5 or 6 inches and often a 3-inch pattern will do well. They should be dressed with lots of Mylar flash — I prefer silver, gold, copper, or a mix of these. One underwater fly I would never be without is a simple black rabbit strip 4 inches long and 3/8-inch wide attached to a 1/0 hook. I put 1/24-ounce lead eyes on some, and I leave the others unweighted. They look awful during the retrieve, but wherever there are leeches in a lake — and most of these northern lakes have them — this fly is among the most deadly. It has caught me several pike over 20 pounds. On the surface a Gartside Gurgler or popping bug will draw some hair-raising strikes.

For grayling, #12–#18 caddis nymph imitations work well. For dry-fly fishing use a brown or gray Elk Hair caddis in size #12–#16.

If the water surface temperature is in the low 50° F range (usually late June and very early July), lake trout will be on the rock piles that litter the lakes. Some of the boulder fields are within inches of the surface but rise from the lake floor from maybe 100 feet below. Fish the shallows with a sinking line and a 4–6 inch silvery baitfish imitation, such as a Sal-Mar-Mac or Lefty's Deceiver. If the lake surface warms above 50° F the fish will start to drop deep. The guides use excellent depth finders to locate the fish and then a lead core shooting head attached to a big, brightly-colored, weighted streamer.

Much of the northern pike fishing in late June and early July is sight fishing where you see the fish and then make the cast. Later as the bays warm the fish tend to be deeper. Since pike are the largest predators in these remote northern lakes, they fear nothing — including you and your boat. Long casts are not necessary and many huge pike can be caught with casts that barely reach 40 feet.

Finally, what also brings me back to the Gangler's North Seal River Lodge is the true wilderness. You often see wolves and many of their tracks on the shoreline or a moose cow feeding on the lily pads with her calf. Bear tracks are everywhere. What appears to be cleared power line right-of-ways in the spruce forest are actually the paths that thousands of migrating caribou make in their southern and northern migrations. This is a true wilderness and it has a special appeal for me that no other fishing destination can offer.

CHAPTER FOUR

THE WEST

ROARING FORK AND FRYING PAN RIVERS
Colorado

Roaring Fork River

The Roaring Fork River is considered to be among Colorado's most important and challenging trout rivers. Certainly, the river rises in some of the most alluring high mountain country in the state, with its headwaters coming off the great flanks of Independence Pass (12,000 feet) and running down to the high meadow country above the town of Aspen.

The Roaring Fork above Aspen is barely a river at all, but more a small high-country stream. From Independence Pass down to Difficult Campground, the stream drops some 4,000 feet in elevation, and has only a few sections that one would deem fishable. Just above Aspen, the stream flows through a meadow section called the Northstar Preserve. This series of meanders and undercut banks holds a population of brookies, rainbows, and browns in only the 8 to 12-inch range, but the occasional 16 to 20-inch brown can also be found there.

Below Aspen, the river moves through a narrow canyon for almost six miles, running toward Upper Woody Creek Bridge. The Roaring Fork moves powerfully through this canyon choked with fallen rocks, and is designated here as wild trout water (flies only, and all trout must be returned to the river). It is open to fly fishermen for the entire six-mile stretch.

From Aspen, the best way to get along the Roaring Fork is from the west end of town, at Slaughterhouse Bridge, which is north down Cemetery Lane. There is parking near the bridge. There is excellent fishing either way you want to go, downstream or up. Many fly fishermen like to hike well downstream and then fish back up toward the bridge; others like to fish from the bridge upstream, back toward town.

Access from the other end of the canyon is from Upper Woody Creek Bridge, which can be reached by taking Highway 82 going west of Aspen and turning at the Woody Creek Canyon sign. Again, there is plenty of parking near the bridge. The river downstream from Upper Woody Creek Bridge holds its share of trout as well. While the river broadens, it remains fast.

At Basalt, the Roaring Fork mingles with another of Colorado's great trout rivers, the Frying Pan. Where the rivers join, the water slows and becomes deeper. Near Basalt, there are two miles of public water, from Bypass Bridge West to Bypass Bridge East, which offers some fine fishing, including the chance to take Colorado whitefish, as well as trout.

Down below the town of Carbondale, the Roaring Fork continues and tumbles over an entire wondrous series of sloping terraces, the oldest of which majestically rises almost 1,000 feet above the valley floor. Each of these old terraces represents an ancient flood plain that was once the floor of this sprawling valley.

Regulation changes on the river, coupled with a decrease in siltation as a result of the closure of the mining activities on the Crystal River, have greatly improved the

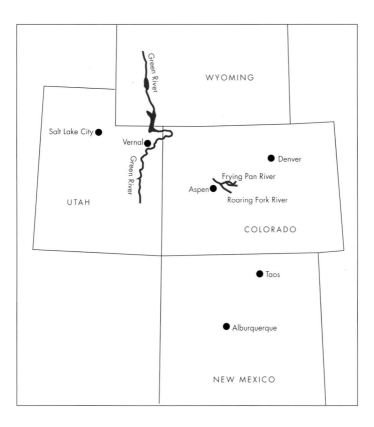

fishing on the lower Roaring Fork between Basalt and Glenwood Springs. It may now be one of the most under-rated trout fisheries in the country.

On the lower Roaring Fork, the section of river from Carbondale to Glenwood Springs fishes better than the section from Basalt to Carbondale. There are solid populations of large browns and rainbows, as well as cutthroats going as large as 20 inches. And the hatches here will rival any other section of the river. This section of river is best fished from a drift boat, as much of the land is private, and the fish, who tend to hold close into the banks, can be better reached with a presentation cast from the middle of the river.

The Roaring Fork is an excellent trout fishery, with a healthy and diverse population of trout and other aquatic life, including a wide range of aquatic insects. Long known for its blizzard caddis hatches, the Roaring Fork also supports a large population of Green Drake mayflies. The emergence of these *Ephemerella* mayflies (#10 to #12) starts during late June in Glenwood Springs, and spends the next month working its way toward Basalt. Golden Stoneflies and nymphs are almost sure things during the summer months as well, and large attractor patterns can be good bets then — especially between Carbondale and Glenwood Springs.

In early spring, beginning perhaps in late April, caddisflies are the dominant insects coming off the river, and their hatches can be prodigious. A wide array of caddisfly patterns works well on the Roaring Fork, in colors from black to soft tan (from #10 to #16). Mayflies work well in the evenings, just at sunset and after. On the Aspen and Basalt sections of the river, it is also prudent to have on hand a selection of Adams, Elk-Hair Caddis, Yellow Humpy, and Irresistible patterns (from #10 to #20).

The Roaring Fork is a productive fishery year-round. During winter, the section from Basalt to Glenwood Springs fishes best, generally with nymphs from late January to early February, then later becoming amenable to a variety of midge imitations.

Frying Pan River

From its headwaters in the high mountains, much of the heavy water flow of the Frying Pan is diverted into the Boustead and Carlton tunnels, which take the water across the Continental Divide and dump it into the Arkansas River. Despite this diversion, there remain several sections of the Frying Pan that are counted among the best trout fisheries in Colorado.

The Frying Pan above Ruedi Dam can provide some absolutely enchanting small-stream, high-country fly fishing. Indeed, on many days, four species of trout (rainbow, brown, cutthroat, and brook) can be caught here. And the meadow section just above Chapman Campground is a collection of oxbows and undercut banks that hold some truly fine brown trout as large as five to seven pounds, although, of course, the big guys tend to be nocturnal during the summer months.

The Frying Pan below Ruedi Dam has gained an international reputation for its large trout and extremely friendly and intimate ambiance. This four-mile run varies from swift pocket water to almost spring-creek style meanders and grassbeds. And while there are plenty of trout here, there are plenty of fly fishermen too.

The Basalt section of the Frying Pan covers more than 14 miles, and a fly fisherman could easily burn a month fishing these waters without ever fishing the same location twice. The river is cold and wide and swift and can be waded along its entire length.

Like the Roaring Fork, the aquatic life in the Frying Pan is rich, including wonderful hatches of midges, mayflies, caddisflies, and a fabled Green Drake hatch. This large olive mayfly begins its emergence in the water around Basalt during mid-July, and works its way upstream towards the dam where it hatches well until the latter part of September.

Pale Morning Duns also hatch at this time on the Frying Pan. Spring and fall can produce extremely heavy hatches of *Baetis* mayflies (#20 to #22). Productive nymph patterns are the Pheasant Tail, Prince, and Buckskin (#16 to #20).

GREEN RIVER
Wyoming and Utah

The headwaters of three of the West's great rivers are found in Wyoming. Out of its rugged, breathtakingly beautiful high mountain country flow the Colorado, the Missouri, and the Columbia rivers. Within the drainages of these three mighty rivers is some of the most pristine trout country and trout water to be found anywhere. In Wyoming, there are trout rivers and lakes that are as wild today as they were at the end of the last Ice Age.

More than 20,000 miles of trout streams cut, coil, meander, undulate across Wyoming. Great trout rivers cascade down through eroded mountain canyons, wander through high country meadows. There are more than 5,000 cold blue-water trout lakes scattered through the high mountain country and down below in the wide, sprawling basins.

Wyoming's wild waters are home to more than 80 species of fish, of which 21 are considered gamefish. Of these, the most popular are the six species of trout that populate Wyoming's rivers and lakes — brook trout and brown trout, lake trout, cutthroats, rainbow trout and the rare golden trout.

Famous trout rivers abound in Wyoming's vast wild country. There is the North Platte and its "Miracle Mile" (which is actually six miles long, between the Seminoe and Pathfinder reservoirs near the towns of Casper, Sinclair, and Alcova); the Snake River (famed for its Snake River cutthroat trout), which flows out of Yellowstone National Park; the North Fork of the Shoshone (famed for its population of Yellowstone cutthroat trout); Clarks Fork of the Yellowstone River, northwest of Cody, Wyoming, which offers some of the most beautiful brook and cutthroat fishing to be found anywhere; plus the Salt River and Greys River, which both provide fine fishing for browns, cutthroats and rainbows.

For many fly fishermen, though, talk of fly fishing in Wyoming invariably means fishing the incredible waters of the Green River.

The magnificent Green River flows for more than 200 miles through Wyoming before it empties into the Flaming Gorge Reservoir along the Wyoming-Utah border. Flowing out of the reservoir, the Green then bends through northern Utah and briefly into Colorado before crossing back into Utah where it finally joins the Colorado River.

The Green is as rich in human history as it is in natural history. It has known explorers and trappers, even outlaws. The Green River country was a favorite hideout for Butch Cassidy's Hole-In-the-Wall Gang.

The river begins near the highest point in Wyoming, Gannett Peak, in the Bridger Wilderness above the Green Lakes near Pinedale. The upper section of the river, which covers more than 100 miles from the river's junction with the New Fork River near Big Piney, upstream to the Green Lakes, offers some truly remarkable trout fishing. This long section of the Green has substantial populations of rainbows, cutthroat, and brook trout, with fish of one to two pounds plentiful and common.

Nearly every mile of the upper Green, as it flows through Sublette and Sweetwater counties, down through the Green River valley at the base of the Wind River mountains, is easy to reach and to fish. The Whiskey Grove campground, west and north of Pinedale, puts you on the headwaters of the Green, where it rushes over downed boulders, its waters shaded by overhanging willows. Rainbows ranging from 10 to 14 inches are common in this section of the river, as are small cutthroat trout.

Farther downstream, the Green opens up, and widens — particularly below Warren Bridge on Highway 191. Many fly fishermen prefer to float this section of the river, especially the beautiful and productive eight-mile run from the bridge down to the Daniel Fish Hatchery. Here, and on downstream, large brown trout become more numerous, mixed with rainbows, cutthroats, and an occasional brookie. There are other excellent float trips above Trapper's Point and the stretch of the Green from Trapper's Point to the confluence of the Green River and the New Fork River.

Until 1962 the upper section of the Green offered the river's best fishing. But the construction of the reservoir and dam at Flaming Gorge (in Utah's northeast corner, about a three-and-a-half hour drive from Salt Lake City) changed the nature and character of that section of the Green below the gorge, creating a new and amazingly rich tailwater trout fishery that extends more than 20 miles below Flaming Gorge Dam, from Dutch Town, Utah, to the Colorado border.

Before the construction of the Flaming Gorge Reservoir, the river below the dam site was only marginal trout water. However, the creation of the tailwater fishery below the dam resulted in the Green River becoming the most heavily populated trout river in the country. Studies have shown that along some sections of the river there are a staggering number of fish — as many as 20,000 trout per river mile! Rainbows and cutthroat are the dominant trout here, along with good populations of trophy browns, and some nice brook trout.

Nymphs are the most predictable flies on this lower section of the Green. Local guides generally recommend that nymph presentations be made with a long leader, split shot, and a strike indicator. Their favorite patterns are the Gold-Ribbed Hare's Ear, Pheasant Tail, Prince, Chamois Caddis, Matts Fur, and Red Fox Squirrel (#12 to #20). Also, scud (freshwater shrimp) patterns, in gray, tan, pink, amber, olive and orange (#12 to #20) and large cranefly nymph patterns (#4 to #8) can be productive.

The best streamers are Muddler Minnows, black, olive, and brown Woolly Buggers, dark or light spruce Matukas, egg patterns and San Juan Worms (#6 to #14).

From late spring into early summer (April through June), small (#18 to #22) Blue-Winged Olives, either gray or olive, are usually productive. Light-colored Pale Morning Duns seem to work best as summer takes hold on the river, while, come fall, the trout begin to favor the Blue-Winged Olives again.

Other favorite dry-fly patterns on the Green are some of the old standbys: Royal Wulffs (#10 to #18), cicada imitations (#6 to #10), Parachute Adams (#16 to #20), Griffith's Gnats (#18 to #22), and brown, cream, and black Grizzly Midges (#18 to #22).

During the river's productive summer months, say from mid-July until the end of September, small hoppers, stoneflies, assorted ant patterns — especially the Cinnamon Ant — and various caddisfly patterns also work well.

Mid to late summer is the best time for fishing the upper Green above Flaming Gorge. Indeed, the second half of July is usually when the trout fishing along most of Wyoming's best trout water is at its peak, and the fishing usually stays good until well into fall.

The lower tailwater section of the Green below Flaming Gorge produces best from March through July. But keep in mind, if you plan to fish this lower tailwater section of the Green, that it has become extremely popular. Indeed, like the Madison, the Bighorn, and other renowned western rivers, this section of the Green has, of late, been dismissed by some fly fishermen as having become too crowded for a decent fly-fishing experience, as having become what some disparage as a "fly-fishing zoo." I agree that there is some justification for this assessment. There are crowds on the Green, fishermen as well as swimmers and tube-floaters. But the people invariably congregate on the most accessible and popular sections of the river, and at the most popular times of the year — particularly on summer weekends and holidays.

If you want to avoid them, there's no easy answer. You'll simply have to work at it, either by beating everybody to the river by arriving first, very early in the morning, or by fishing only on weekdays or in the early and late periods of the summer. But I can assure you, given the quality of its trout, it's worth an extra measure of effort to experience the superb fly fishing on this great water.

YELLOWSTONE NATIONAL PARK
Wyoming

For many fly fishermen there is one place that haunts them above all others, a place not only of great fishing, but of great beauty, a country still touched by that ancient wildness that trout and not a few fly fishermen need to survive. That place is the outstanding Yellowstone National Park and the small town of West Yellowstone, with its streets lined with fly-fishing shops, guides, and parties of fly fishermen from around the world, all of them happy and smiling, all of them certain they have arrived at last in a true angler's paradise.

The general season opening for the Yellowstone Park waters each year is from the Saturday before Memorial Day until the first Sunday in November.

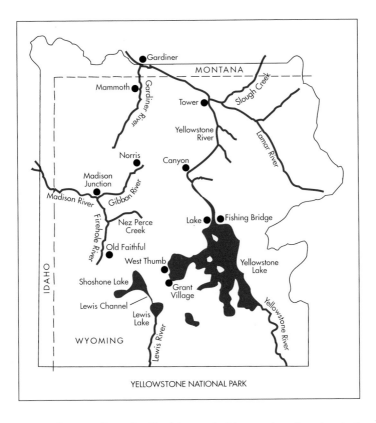

YELLOWSTONE NATIONAL PARK

Understanding the Park's myriad insect hatches is vital for optimal fishing success. Both in terms of variety and quantity, there are huge insect hatches on the rivers in the Park throughout the fishing season. Emergence dates vary, of course, from stream to stream, so it's best to check with a local fly-fishing shop for exact emergence times and places for each of the Park's watersheds that you plan to fish on. Some of the major hatches — but certainly not all — include Little Blue-Winged Olive Duns, Tiny Blue-Winged Olives, Pale Morning Duns, Western Green Drakes, Brown Drakes, Flavs, Gray Drakes, Tricos, Pink

Ladies, black, brown and olive caddisflies, Little Yellow Stoneflies, Golden Stoneflies, Salmon Flies, and midges.

Yellowstone National Park is noted for a great many things, a great many natural wonders, its spectacular beauty, its preserved and protected remnant wildness. Among fly fishermen, it is also noted for its miles and miles of gorgeous trout water, its diverse and grand fly-fishing challenges. There is so much great fishable water here, in fact, that some fortunate Wyoming and Montana anglers literally spend their entire lives exploring and fishing the waters of the Park, and numerous articles and books have been written about it. But the five major fisheries of the Park which every American fly fisherman should try to fish at least once in his lifetime are the Yellowstone, the Firehole, the Madison, Lewis Lake and Channel, and Slough Creek.

Yellowstone River

A number of famous trout rivers move through the Park's vast boundaries, including the much loved Yellowstone River. Like all trout rivers, the Yellowstone is never one river, a river of predictable moods and habits. It is a river that is always greater than the sum of its parts.

On the upper Yellowstone is Buffalo Ford, one of the river's most talked about fishing spots. Buffalo Ford is unusually easy to get to. The parking area is only a matter of yards from the river's edge. And this is a section of the Yellowstone full of a staggering number of cutthroat trout, the handsome subspecies known as the Yellowstone cutthroat (Salmo clarki bouvieri). The cutthroat found at Buffalo Ford can be as large as 14 to 16 inches.

At Buffalo Ford, the Yellowstone shows an easy mood, an agreeable nature, but the river changes drastically near its headwaters, which can only be reached either by hiking in through the backcountry or by way of a canoe trip across Yellowstone Lake. It is a trip that is well worth the effort. The river's headwaters are located near the southern boundary of Yellowstone National Park, and as it flows into and then out of Lake Yellowstone, the river tends to dominate the northern section of the Park. This section of the upper Yellowstone offers the fly fisherman one of the country's largest and purest natural cutthroat trout fisheries.

At its headwaters, there is as yet no main channel to the Yellowstone. Instead, the river is actually a radiating band of small rivers meandering through the lush high country meadows. The trout are smaller than at Buffalo Ford, but there are plenty of them, and the countryside is almost unspeakably magnificent.

The Yellowstone enters the sprawl of Lake Yellowstone from the east (what is called the Eastern Arm). The lake, too, offers a healthy population of Yellowstone cutthroat. In the lake, as in the river, small cutthroats and cutts up to 18 inches attack flies with a stunning ferocity.

The most popular section of the Yellowstone is the six-mile run from the point where the river leaves the lake at Fishing Bridge to Sulphur Caldron. This entire section of the river is operated as a no-kill section, and the cutthroat thrive here, some reaching sizes of 20 inches or more. The average size of these Yellowstone cutthroat, though, is about 16 inches, and it is not uncommon, during a day's worth of splendid fishing, to take and release 20 trout from this section of the river.

From Sulphur Caldron to where Alum Creek joins the river, the Yellowstone is operated as a wildlife sanctuary and is closed to fishing. Along this stretch of the river there are not only trout, but moose and elk, buffalo, deer, and mule deer grazing along the banks of the river.

Further downstream, below the lovely Yellowstone Falls, is the Grand Canyon of the Yellowstone, where the ragged cliffs loom 1,000 feet above the river. Fishing is allowed, but available only to those anglers who are in extremely good physical condition and who are skilled backcountry hikers with some knowledge and experience in mountain climbing.

One less difficult way to experience not only the beauty of this part of the Yellowstone but its often excellent cutthroat trout fishing, is to go farther downstream and take the somewhat easier trek into Black Canyon. While it is an easy walk, this hike to the river, which can be from one to four miles, depending upon where you start, is seldom taken by most anglers, which may be part of the reason why those fly fishermen who fish the Black Canyon section of the Yellowstone regularly think it offers the best cutthroat trout fishing to be found anywhere along the river.

Most fly fishermen who hike into the canyon stay at the Lava Creek campgrounds. An easy trail into the canyon is nearby, off Old Towers Falls Road.

The trip into Black Canyon can be made in a day, but to do so means rushing things, including the fishing. But an overnight trip into the canyon usually allows you to sample the fishing in late afternoon and early twilight, and again in the long, bright, productive morning hours. The Black Canyon stretch of the Yellowstone River covers about 20 miles of wild, pristine river, and actually marks the end of the river's truly superb cutthroat trout fishing.

Among fly fishermen, the upper section of the Yellowstone continues to be the most fished section of the river. Yes, there are crowds, and at times the crowds are maddening, but the crowds, or at least the bulk of them, can be avoided with a little planning. The Yellowstone is an active trout river throughout the season, from early spring into early fall. However, most of the tourists to the Park do not arrive until early summer, and the crowds are pretty much gone after Labor Day. So many experienced Yellowstone anglers plan their fishing for the period after Labor Day until the Park closes in early November.

As with all of the extremely popular western trout rivers, with some advance planning and maybe a bit of hiking, the crowds on the Yellowstone can be avoided, or they can simply be taken as part of the experience of fishing the river. As crowded as it becomes, for example, Buffalo Ford has yielded many a fine cutthroat trout over the years, and a great many lifelong angling friendships have been started there as well.

Beginning with opening day on the river, (opening day on the section of the river above Yellowstone Falls is not until the 15th of July), the hatches are in full measure and the trout are feeding fiercely. Any number of mayfly patterns can prove to be very successful, as are caddisfly and large stonefly imitations.

The Salmon Fly and Golden Stonefly hatches on the Yellowstone are spectacular. Fish the canyon area prior to July 15th, and then above the canyon after that section of the river opens. Fish will come up to pattern imitations during most of July, especially on the east bank of the river upstream from Chittenden Bridge and at LeHardy Rapids. A great pattern is an Orange Stimulator (#10 to #12).

Firehole River

Another of the famous trout rivers of Yellowstone National Park is the Firehole River. The Firehole just may be the most unique of the country's many trout rivers, in that it is a river that is spawned mainly from hot springs. Even so, the river's trout population has, over time, adapted to the river's steamy character. So have the many diverse forms of life that live along the river, including a rich population of aquatic and terrestrial insects.

Twice a year, the waters of the Firehole boil with more than temperature; they can boil with trout. May is usually the first good month on the river. The water still holds some of the winter's chill, though it is warm enough for insect and trout activity. During the last week of May and perhaps for a time into early June, the Firehole becomes a wondrous stretch of trout water. Once true summer takes hold, however, the river changes mood, boils and bubbles, and does not attract many trout or fly fishermen until it again begins to change, usually from mid-August into September, when the banks along the river are alive with grasshoppers and the trout are once again feeding.

If the Firehole itself goes into the doldrums during the long, hot summer months, many of its tributaries do remain cool enough throughout the season for trout fishing. Indeed, during the summer months, when the Firehole really heats up, large, thick knots of trout can be found where the cooler waters of its tributaries empty into the river. But great caution has to be used when trying to fish among the spooky trout in these waters. One mistake is likely to send the whole congregation into hiding. Streamers and hoppers at sundown and early twilight usually work well, both from the banks near these feeder streams and in the main channel of the Firehole where some big trout like to stay, regardless of the warming temperatures.

Fly fishing the Firehole always demands concentration and precise casts using long leaders (6X and 7X) and small (#16 to #20) flies. Small wet flies, nymphs, and midge pupae have also proved productive on the haunting, steaming waters of the Firehole. Soft-hackle patterns that match the hatch are excellent, as are Pale Morning Duns; Pale Evening Duns (yellow and herl); various caddis patterns; Serendipity, Ram and Z-Wing patterns (in brown, tan, olive and peacock); midges (peacock and herl); Blue-Winged Olives (olive and herl); and Pheasant Tail Nymphs.

Generally, on the Firehole the browns will hang tight on the banks, and the rainbows will hold in the middle runs. Due to the varying current speeds in this spring creek, one of the best ways to fish the Firehole is to fish an emerger on a downstream quarter-cast so that the current will swing the fly around. Good-sized browns and rainbows will come off the bottom to smack it.

Madison River

The Firehole and the Gibbon join to form perhaps the Park's most famous trout river, one of the most famous trout rivers in the world, the Madison. From the junction of the Firehole and the Gibbon, for nearly 100 miles downstream, the Madison offers consistently excellent trout fishing.

Access is easy, being just inside the West Yellowstone entrance. A well-maintained road just over a quarter-mile east of the entrance will bring you right down to Barn's Pools on the lower section of the Madison. The fishing is excellent here, especially from Beaver Meadows and Barn's Pools upstream, as the river broadens and slows, and then flows through the beautiful mountain meadows. Various caddisflies patterns generally work well all through the summer, as do Western Green Drakes, and fly patterns imitating *Ephemerella* and *Drunella* mayflies. Evenings along this stretch of the river can bring clouds of spinners. Big wet flies, stoneflies, and nymphs all work well along the river as the day's sunlight fades.

Lewis Lake and Channel

Most fly fishermen have heard of the excellent trout fishing to be found within the Park on Lewis Lake. Fewer have heard of what can be the incredible trout fishing to be found along the Lewis Channel, which is that section of the Lewis River between Lewis Lake and Shoshone Lake in the south-central part of Yellowstone National Park. Access is by way of the South Entrance Road and Lewis Lake.

Not a few anglers believe that Lewis Channel offers the best autumn fishing in the Park. This is brown trout water. Big browns frequent both the Lewis and Shoshone lakes, and the trout from both lakes move into the channel to spawn beginning about the second week in September. The spawning browns, which are bigger fish, will usually take big streamers (#4 to #2/0), Marabou Muddlers, and various leech patterns.

In fact, because of this spawning activity, Lewis Channel is closed to all fishermen after October 15th. Even though fall is the best time for the spawning fish, the resident browns of Lewis Channel can be fished almost anytime, from late spring to early winter. When they are feeding, these browns, from 15 to 20 inches, have a special fondness for big mayflies and caddisflies.

On Lewis (and Shoshone) Lake, spring is an excellent time to fish for the lake's big Mackinaw trout during "ice out," the period from opening of the water in late May to June 20th. At this time, it is not unusual to capture fish in the 15 to 20-pound range.

Slough Creek

Slough Creek flows through the northeastern part of the Park, and if you are willing to invest a 30-minute hike to get to its best trout water, you will not be disappointed.

From early July into September, this meadow run of Slough Creek can be pulsing with feeding cutthroat, from 12 to 20 inches. A U.S. Park Service study once revealed that along this meadow section of Slough Creek the average angler took five trout an hour.

Three Other Yellowstone Destinations

If you're willing to take a short hike, go east at Tower to Agate Creek Camp where it runs into the Yellowstone. This is an excellent piece of water, with cutthroats and rainbows at an average size of 18 inches.

Or park or camp at Tower Campground and hike up Tower Creek for about 30 minutes for great solitude and quality fishing. The ancestors of the 13 to 17-inch rainbows that inhabit this stretch of water were put there when Dwight Eisenhower was president of the United States, and he fished for them, too.

Or in the fall — late September and all of October — fish the Gardiner River. Brown trout come up into this water from the Yellowstone River, and can be taken on streamers, nymphs, or imitations of the river's excellent Blue-Winged Olive and Pale Morning Dun hatches.

BIGHORN RIVER

Montana

Among almost any fly fisherman's pantheon of Montana blue-ribbon trout water is the beautiful Bighorn River. Open to fishing only since a Supreme Court decision in 1981 (disputes with the Indians closed the river in 1975), the Bighorn has already become legendary for its trout fishing, and especially for its highly praised nymph and streamer fishing.

Over the years, however, fly fishermen who have fished the Bighorn, who have become addicted to it, and who keep returning to its waters again and again have also discovered that the Bighorn may well be one of the best dry-fly trout streams in the country. At its best, many believe the Bighorn is easily as challenging and productive as Idaho's superb dry-fly trout stream, Silver Creek.

The headwaters of the Bighorn are in the high, rugged country of Wyoming's Wind River range, in the area near Thermopolis, Wyoming. From there, the Bighorn flows north until it empties into the Yellowstone River. The Bighorn flows through the deeply magnificent basin country of southeast Montana, winding down through the Crow Indian Reservation and the town of Fort Smith, about 85 miles east of Billings.

It is a country that seems as endless as the stretch of Montana's vast blue skies. Once in the basin, the bright waters of the Bighorn often reflect the distant flanks of the Bighorn Mountains where the river begins. Farther to the west are the humpbacked ridges of the Pryor Mountains, and farther still the high peaks of the Beartooth Mountains leave a ragged purple tear across the horizon.

As a trout river, the Bighorn has something of an unnatural history. Before 1965, when the Bighorn Lake project and the Yellowtail Dam were completed, the river was naturally a warm-water river below Lovell, Wyoming, and as such it held no charm either for trout or for trout anglers. The construction of the Yellowtail Dam and the creation of the lake, however, changed the basic nature of the river from warm to cold water, a change that eventually resulted in the creation of one of the country's most famous tailwater trout rivers.

The constant rush of tailwater from Yellowtail Dam cools the waters of the Bighorn most effectively, especially

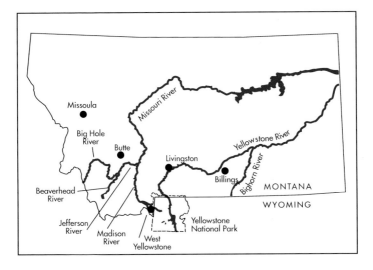

during the scorching summer months. The river's water flow, like the temperature, is nearly constant, and the river water is wonderfully crystal clear and rich in nutrients released into the water by the flooding of its limestone canyons, nutrients that in turn create an abundance of aquatic insects. The Bighorn has actually taken on many of the lovely qualities of a spring creek, and does not freeze over during the winter months.

When the river became a tailwater fishery, while neither the quality nor the quantity of its insect populations and hatches were altered, the cycle of its hatches were. Insects that would normally hatch, say, in early summer, on rivers like the Madison, do not hatch on the Bighorn until August. From the fly fisherman's perspective, this quirk in the rhythm of the river's hatches is a benefit, providing the fishery with a longer dry-fly season — one running from late July all the way through early fall — with the best months for the dry fly being from late July until the middle of September.

The first rush of warmth in May brings small midges and *Baetis* mayflies, and the dry-fly fishing is superb. After the early midge and mayfly hatches, nymphs and streamers work well. With warmer water, Yellow Stoneflies and Pale Morning Duns become ever more productive. Late July is the time for caddisflies, beginning with tiny black caddisflies. Of course, the best caddisfly fishing comes with the late afternoon times, dusk and twilight, with nymphs being the best during the bright afternoons.

While fly fishermen are always arguing about the incredible trout waters of Montana, bickering about which rivers are the best, there seems to be little disagreement among them about the Bighorn. It is consistently mentioned as being perhaps the most productive trout river in Montana, which is saying a great deal indeed. Figures vary, naturally, but it is perhaps safe to say that the trout population of the Bighorn contains as many as 2,500 brown trout per river mile, with at least a quarter of those going three pounds or better. Bighorn rainbows are not as abundant as the browns, but they can be just as challenging. Too, they can grow to substantial size. The record books show at least one rainbow trout of more than 15 pounds being taken on the Bighorn. The best fishing on the river is generally below Yellowtail Dam, near Fort Smith, Montana.

When conditions are right, even anglers who choose to fish only dry flies can often take more than a dozen big browns and rainbows a day, all of them measuring between 14 to 20 inches, and most of them taken from along the river's many weedbeds, at the edge of the current in the fast water, near drop-offs, and especially at the head of the river's many long pools.

In its journey toward the Yellowstone River, the Bighorn crosses the Crow Indian Reservation, where access to the river for trout fishing is limited. Because most of the land on both sides of the river is privately owned, no camping is permitted. The best way to fish this section of the Bighorn, then, is by boat. There are numerous day float trips from Afterbay Dam down through this part of the river. Most anglers who come to float-fish the Bighorn stay in nearby Fort Smith.

Bighorn trout can frequently be seen moving in small schools, their backs breaking the surface of the water, glistening in the sun. Like all wild trout, they are maddeningly suspicious, wary, and selective. Bighorn insect hatches can be intense. Even during the thickest hatch, though, taking a Bighorn trout takes a precise cast and delicate presentation. Due to the abundance of food, the fish simply will not bother to take a fly that is poorly cast and off the mark. In fact, often the only way to get a Bighorn trout to strike is to put the fly right on the trout's nose.

The Bighorn's flow and the aggressive nature of its trout make it a dry-fly fisherman's dream. Conditions for fishing the dry fly are often near perfect. The river's bigger trout, though, usually prove to be beyond the tactics of dry-fly fishing. More often than not, the only thing that will tempt these big trout are the larger streamers, fished on sinking lines that will get the streamers down into the current fast.

The strike of the Bighorn trout, when it comes, can be savage, and the fish are noted for their fight, especially the browns, who most unusually, have great jumping ability. It is not uncommon for these trout to burn through 75 yards of line. Consequently, reel selection is an important matter when fishing the Bighorn. When you are going after the river's big trout, a reel that can handle the fly line plus at least a hundred yards of backing, and handle it well, is essential.

For many dedicated Bighorn anglers, October is the best fishing month, The trees along the river are already deep in color and by evening, there is a cool wind coming off the mountains. Overhead at dusk, there is the sound of wings on the wind, geese and ducks heading south. Then the Montana big sky is an infinite mix of soft colors, of evening rising and day receding, and the only sounds are that of the cool October wind and of the Bighorn, its waters trilling in the rising darkness.

YELLOWSTONE RIVER — BEYOND THE PARK
Montana

While that portion of the Yellowstone lying within the boundaries of Yellowstone National Park offers some incredible trout fishing, which in turn draws an incredible number of fly fishermen, that section of the Yellowstone beyond Park boundaries is trout water extraordinary. Neither the river nor its great trout end, of course, at the Park boundary. It does not suddenly change and become a different river, at least not at once.

From the boundary of the Park to Reed Point, there remain 125 miles of blue-ribbon trout water. More importantly, at least to the fly fisherman seeking a quieter, less crowded Yellowstone experience, this part of the river rarely draws the flocks of anglers that regularly descend on the Park.

From Reed Point to Billings, the river still offers trout, but not consistently or in size or numbers. After Billings, the Yellowstone becomes a warm-water fishery, not amenable to meaningful trout populations.

Near Gardiner, there is good early season fishing on the Salmon Fly hatch, but as the season progresses, fishing on this section of the river falls off. Below Gardiner, cutthroat trout no longer dominate the Yellowstone. Instead, there are more brown trout, rainbows, and whitefish. Likewise, for bigger trout the fishing can be spectacular along the 50 miles of river from Yankee Jim Canyon to Livingston and Springdale, a section which includes the incredible beauty of Paradise Valley and magnificent views of the Gallatin and Absaroka mountains.

Fishing on the river is especially good near Livingston. The largest fish and best concentrations of browns and rainbows are to be found there. The best stretch of water in this section is between Mill Creek (Pray Bridge) down through Livingston to the bridge at Highway 89.

Beyond Livingston, the Yellowstone bends to the east, flowing toward Big Timber and Billings and the angling remains extraordinarily good, with endless opportunities for wading the edges of riffles, pools, and shoals as the river widens and becomes far more unpredictable. The stretch of river between Springdale and Laurel is one of the least crowded areas on the Yellowstone, and while there are fewer trout here, what trout there are tend to be bigger and more of a challenge.

Access to the Yellowstone is much easier and less restricted outside the Park. There are numerous state Fish and Game access points, including, for instance, Joe Brown Access at the head of Yankee Jim Canyon. The same is true of the river as it flows north towards Livingston and then to Springdale, Big Timber, and Laurel.

To experience as much of the Yellowstone as possible, many anglers float portions of the river, especially the lower river, much of which can only be reached by boat.

The entire lower river is catch-and-release on cutthroats, and this has considerably improved the chances for catching a big one.

Throughout its course, the Yellowstone remains a hatch river, principally dry-fly water, with the truly good fishing fueled by the cycle of river hatches running from spring well into fall. The major difference between the upper and lower Yellowstone is probably that the lower river is not marked by the same great hatches as the upper reaches of the river. There are hatches on the lower river, of course, only they are smaller and less dramatic in nature. Even so, the lower Yellowstone has a fine population of the same famous Yellowstone mix of trout, from the fierce cutthroats to rainbows, browns, and hybrids, though the lower river may not hold as many trout as the upper Yellowstone. Numbers aside, this section of the river does hold big trout, with some of the cutthroats going to five pounds, and significant numbers of rainbows and browns weighing as much as 10 pounds.

As with that part of the river in the Park, the best time on the lower reaches of the Yellowstone begins in early July with the Salmon Fly hatch and continues well into September and October. Indeed, the later months, August and September especially, are often the best months on the Yellowstone, especially for dry-fly fishing with hoppers and attractor patterns.

There is also outstanding fishing on the Yellowstone before the snow run-off in the period from March to May. Good early hatches of midges and *Baetis* mayflies, and nymph fishing, provide a lot of action. Just before run-off, in late April and early May, the Yellowstone gets its terrific "Mother's Day caddis hatch," and it is the finest dry-fly fishing of the entire season. Big fish are rising everywhere, and black and brown caddisflies blanket the river.

Throughout the summer months, fly selections for the Yellowstone, upper and lower, should include Salmon Flies (#6 and #8), tan and black caddisflies (#12 to #18), as well as Golden Stoneflies, Little Blue-Winged Olives, Little Yellow Stoneflies (#8 to #16), Western Green Drakes, Gray Drakes, Tricos, and Western Quill Gordons.

In July and thereafter, be sure to have plenty of hopper patterns and attractor patterns such as Royal Wulffs, Trudes, Humpys and Stimulators. Late September through November is the time to throw streamer patterns — Muddler Minnows, Spruce Flies, and Woolly Buggers — if you are after big browns.

Anyone fishing the Yellowstone near Livingston should try to spend a day, as well, on one of the famous private spring creeks of Paradise Valley, Armstrong's, DePuy's, and Nelson's. But call a local fly shop well before your trip to make a reservation, as these small creeks have rod limits, and are generally booked up far in advance of the season.

MADISON RIVER

Montana

Long considered one of the preeminent fly-fishing rivers in the world, the Madison is thick with rainbows and browns, and most of the time there is splendid fishing for its entire length, from where the river begins at Madison Junction in Yellowstone National Park to Three Forks.

At one time in its long history, the Madison was a stocked trout stream. The stocking program was stopped, though, in the 1970s and the Madison's wild trout population, from Quake Lake to Ennis Lake, in Ennis, quickly recovered. Thus ended the Madison's one and only experimental brush, so far, with hatchery trout.

The Madison is a long meandering sleeve of bright blue-green water, a river that is wide and of boisterous character. It begins in the Wyoming section of Yellowstone National Park (this 14-mile section of the Madison that lies within the boundaries of the Park is one of the loveliest parts of the river) and flows northwest into Montana; first into Hebgen Lake and then Earthquake Lake (locally, just "Quake Lake").

Flowing out of Quake Lake, the Madison turns in a more northerly direction, accompanied by the path of U.S. Route 287, passing through the small towns of Cameron and Ennis, and then north of Ennis empties into Ennis Lake, home of the Madison Dam. Below the dam is the rugged country of Bear Trap Canyon. Beyond the canyon, the river widens and slows until it joins with the Gallatin and Jefferson rivers near Three Forks, Montana, to form the Missouri River.

For most of its journey, the Madison River rips and snorts through Madison Valley. Its waters move at a regular and vigorous rhythm, with many currents, seams, pockets, pools and riffles.

From the angler's perspective, the Madison can be handily divided into three sections: the upper Madison (the high quality trout water extending 50 miles from Quake Lake to Varney Bridge); the middle Madison (from Varney Bridge to Ennis); and the lower Madison (which is essentially Ennis Lake down to Three Forks). The best trout section of the river is the upper Madison. But some of the largest fish in the river have been caught in the section from Varney Bridge downstream.

While the Madison has become as well known for its crowds of fly fishermen as for its trout and the allure of its splendid water, there are still places along the river where a fly fisherman can find solitude, enjoying only the company of the river and its trout. This is especially true as the river moves through Bear Trap Canyon, running about 30 or more miles, from below Ennis Lake to Three Forks.

There are only two ways to get into Bear Trap Canyon, either by guided boat or on foot. Either way, there is considerable effort involved. Even so, the fishing down through this wild eroded canyon of the Madison can often be excellent, except during the hot months of July and August when the water warms up too much. One cautionary note: *do not attempt to float Bear Trap Canyon on your own. Some of its white-water sections are extremely dangerous — even deadly.*

Trout size along the Madison is fairly consistent. Rainbows of about 16 inches or so are common. The river's brown trout population is a little larger. The trout found in the river below the lake, among the fast, rock-strewn waters of Bear Trap Canyon, are just as challenging and can often be a great deal bigger.

Ennis Lake itself has an outstanding population of rainbow trout, but because anglers come to fish the more popular stretches of the Madison, the lake gets little fishing pressure. As the river enters the lake, it breaks into several long, slow narrow channels, each one becoming a small, lovely trout stream as it runs a mile before finally mingling with the lake. The trout fishing along these quiet channels above the lake is not only productive, but a great deal of fun.

Besides Ennis Lake, there are several other lakes near the Madison that are full of trout, including trout that tip the scales at 20 pounds or better. Wade Lake, Hidden Lake, Elk Lake, and Cliff Lake are all deep, cold, volcanic lakes near the upper Madison. Hidden Lake can only be reached by foot. The hike is beautiful. The fishing is consistently amazing.

When in Madison River country, if time permits, the angler ought to try and fish the lesser known, but rich waters, of some of the river's tributaries, the South Fork of the Madison, as well as Duck Creek, Cougar Creek, and Grayling Creek, including the waters of the streams that are inside the boundaries of Yellowstone National Park.

The most popular section of the Madison continues to be that part of the river that runs from Ennis to Quake Lake, which takes its name from an earthquake that shook the region in 1959. The quake dramatically changed the topography of the river. Several miles of the Madison, that section up near Hebgen Lake, were actually lost, collapsing into the newly formed and named Quake Lake. This section of the river still bears ugly scars. Some of the scar tissue is natural, the legacy of the earthquake, and some of it is unnatural, the legacy of the Army Corps of Engineers. But even if the scenery along this section of the river is not as stunning as the rest of the river, the fishing here remains superb.

As May eases into the warming days of June, crowds of fly fishermen, anticipating the river's spectacular stonefly hatch, descend on the river. (Along the Madison, the stonefly hatch is called the Salmon Fly hatch.) While the hatch can come at almost anytime after early June, usually it does not reach its peak until the last week of June and the first days of July. During these weeks, the river's big trout are apt to hit large flies that come closest to matching the size, look, texture, and motion of hatching stoneflies.

However, the more predictable and consistent hatches on the Madison are those of its various caddisflies. These hatches offer superb fishing from June through early September. In addition to the standard Elk-Hair Caddis, the X-Caddis pattern, which simulates an escaping adult, is extremely effective when fished in the surface film. The Z-Wing Emerger has also proven to be effective early and late in the season, fished as a dropper. When the air warms during July and August, early morning and evening spinner falls of such insects as Pale Morning Duns do not get the attention they rightfully deserve. The Z-Wing Spinner (Rusty and Olive/Cream) is a productive imitation.

Other hatches occur throughout the summer and early fall along the river, including swarms of caddisflies, Pale Morning Duns, Flavs, Blue-Winged Olives (*Baetis*), mayflies and flying ants. And in the softening sunlight and cooler days of August and September, the high meadows along the river rattle with grasshoppers, and the fishing, already legendary, becomes instantly fabled, quite extraordinary. Beetle imitations can also achieve superb results throughout the summer. The standard and productive streamer patterns on the Madison are Woolly Buggers (#4 to #8), Bitch Creeks (#6 to #8), and Brown Girdle Bugs (#6 to #8).

Many non-resident anglers fish the Madison by drift boat with guides booked from a number of fly shops located along the river, in West Yellowstone, and in Ennis. Wading is of course possible and a popular way to fish the river. But the Madison is heavy-river, with a bouldery and slippery bottom, and care needs to be exercised by the newcomer. Whether working from a drift boat or wading, the most effective technique for fishing the Madison, in the opinion of many local guides, is always to fish the banks first, before working out into midstream to cover its holes and runs. This appears to be particularly sound reasoning on a river like the Madison which is so difficult to wade anyway.

Because of its great and certainly deserved reputation as being one of the great trout rivers of the world, the Madison continues to grow in popularity. With this swelling popularity have come increasing crowds of anglers and a dramatic increase in fishing pressure, particularly, of course, in the summer months. But so far, the Madison has shown a remarkable resiliency. Because the river offers miles and miles of excellent trout fishing (sections of the river also offer grayling and mountain whitefish), the fishing pressure on the river as a whole has been absorbed with almost no loss of either the river's great fishing or its magnificent beauty.

The Madison is also an excellent fishery in the fall, from September to November, when the fishing pressure has greatly diminished; and in the spring, from April to June, before the snow run-off begins and before most anglers have arrived. In the fall, streamers and nymphs work well, as do imitations of the season's Blue Dun and Trico hatches. Midges hatch in the spring. Of course, during these times, you can expect to encounter some foul weather: after all, this is Montana. But with the superlative rough weather clothing available today, these early and late months are certainly worth consideration by the serious fly fisherman.

MISSOURI RIVER

Montana

The Missouri is among those rivers that have marked the nation's character and its history, a river of great cultural and historical importance. A big, broad-shouldered river, the Missouri offers great stretches of fly-fishing water that in some respects resemble a huge spring creek, yet with a wide variety of water structure — flat water, riffles, eddies.

Its headwaters form near Three Forks, Montana, where the union of the Jefferson, Madison, and Gallatin rivers form to create the Missouri, which flows north.

Many fly fishermen believe that the best trout water on the Missouri is the 30-mile section of river from Holter

Dam down to Cascade. Within that section, the 16 miles from Holter Dam to the junction of the Dearborn River is simply spectacular. All along these stretches downriver from the dam, there is plenty of clearly marked access.

Others believe that the best trout fishing on the river is near Craig, Montana and Holter Lake. The fishing here is nearly always superb, with the water holding a healthy population of wary brown trout, some going four to five pounds. Trout from 15 to 22 inches are common, but hard to entice, hard to hook. This section of the river, like most of the Missouri, is most often floated with guides who know where to anchor to put fly fishermen close to the river's browns and rainbows (like the browns, the rainbows are trout of size, the average fish between 14 and 15 inches). Even though many anglers prefer floating, the Missouri, for a big river, does offer some easy wading. You do not need a boat to experience the grandeur of the Missouri or the wonder of its trout fishing.

It is not unusual along some of the Missouri's more productive shoals and shallow pools to take more than a dozen rainbows in an hour's time. While this might sound like easy fishing, when it comes to the Missouri, the fly fisherman soon learns that there is no easy fishing and that every trout, every memory, is all the more precious because it has to be worked for, earned. It is a trout river where the angler has to rely as much on skill as luck, on instinct as circumstance. It is a thinking man's river.

Among fly fishermen, the Missouri's importance is newly appreciated and celebrated each year, and especially during the river's famed summer Trico hatch, which is truly one of the country's most famous trout hatches, an event surrounded by as much myth as fact.

The fact is that the hatch often boils off the river in such clouds of insects that fly fishing for trout here is more than difficult and vexing; it is nearly impossible. Desperate to get these swarms of rising trout to at least look at their offerings, local anglers and guides on the Missouri have often been driven to extreme measures. One which seems to have paid off handsomely is the device of tying spinners that actually imitate not a single fly but rather a knot of emerging flies. The Missouri Trico hatch can be that thick, that incredible, that challenging. No wonder fly fishermen begin showing up along the Missouri each summer in mid-July!

Trico hatches usually begin on the Missouri in mid-July, and continue, in various magnitudes, into the early fall. While the Missouri is known and hailed for its Trico hatch, there are other hatches on the river that commonly produce some incredible dry-fly fishing, including caddis-flies, Pale Morning Duns and Pale Evening Duns. In April and again in the fall, often the river is blanketed with Blue-Winged Olives. Indeed, one way to beat the river's bristling Trico crowds is to wait them out, come back to the river in the fall after the crowds have gone, and await the arrival of the Blue-Winged Olives that drift above the river like a shining mist.

As for what to bring to the Missouri: first, steady nerves and plenty of patience.

Then, in April and May (when the most important hatches are midges and *Baetis*), favorite patterns are Griffith's Gnats (#18 to #22), Adams Parachutes and Olive Comparaduns (#16 to #20), and large streamers and cray-fish patterns. Springtime is a good time to go for large browns, particularly on overcast days when the fish seem to be more active.

In June through the latter part of August, there are caddisflies, Pale Morning Duns, and of course, the famous Trico hatches. Popular patterns for the summer season are

Elk-Hair Caddis (#14 to #18), Jim's Caddis Emerger (#14 to #16), Pale Morning Dun Nymphs and Emergers (#14 to #18), Trico Parachutes and Comparaduns, H & L Variants, Adams Parachutes, Trico Spinners (#18 to #20), Parachute and Elk-Hair Hoppers (#8 to #12), Gold-Ribbed Hare's Ear, Olive Flashback, Pheasant Tail, and Zug Bug Nymphs (#12 to #18), and Royal Wulffs and Trudes (#12 to #16).

In September and October, streamer fishing is also particularly good, producing many rainbows and trophy browns. In fact, mid-October to mid-November is probably the best time on the Missouri for a truly big fish. Favorite streamer patterns are the Woolly Bugger, Brown Crystal Bugger, Girdle Bug, Marabou Muddler, and Crayfish (#2 to #6).

BIG HOLE RIVER

Montana

Montana, a land of complicated beauty, still edged in wildness, is marked by a latticework of great trout rivers. For many of these rivers, their reputations came naturally; for others, like the Ruby and the Big Hole, their reputations have been helped along by the efforts of man.

Before its rapid decline in the 1960s, evidently the Big Hole was truly one of Montana's premier trout streams, a river especially revered for its Salmon Fly hatch. But during the late 1950s and early 1960s ranchers began diverting the river for irrigation, a practice that rapidly led to the river's near ruin, leaving it as nothing more than a muddy channel where migrating trout lingered and died.

But later, an enlightened group of ranchers, along with such organizations as the state's Office of Environmental

Quality and local chapters of Trout Unlimited, worked out a solution to the river's woes, forming the Alliance for Montana Waters, which works to maintain Montana ranching and the dignity and quality of its great trout waters.

As the Big Hole regains its health and its stature, it continues to live off its past, a past that covers it with such glory that it often seems a river more of myth than of fact. Today, as the river recovers, it is slowly regaining its fame, a new respect, especially as a brown trout river. Big browns tend to dominate the river — or at least that wonderful section between the towns of Twin Bridges and Divide. While the brown trout population is heaviest in this section of the river, there are rainbows, including some big ones, mixed in with the browns. In the canyon section, from Divide to Melrose, a number of rainbows can be found, but most rainbows to be found in this section average from 14 to 17 inches.

In that section of the river above Divide, the character and mood of the river change dramatically. The numbers of big browns decline, while the numbers of rainbow increase. Brook trout and native grayling are also found in this section of the Big Hole. This section is often called Big Hole Basin, and is marked in spring and summer by what seems an endless sprawl of meadows and freshly mowed hay. Often, the landscape, in every direction, is crowded with patterns of haystacks. It is beautiful country, and it is indeed good news that the Big Hole can, once again, be counted among Montana's great trout rivers.

For those fly fishermen wanting to fish the Big Hole's Salmon Fly hatch, the best time on the river is probably from early to late June, though there have been reports of Salmon Fly hatches on the river as early as mid-May.

When the river's big Salmon Fly hatch is on, the Big Hole is still known to attract quite a crowd of fly fishermen, most of whom float the river. It is not uncommon to arrive at the Big Hole only to find that there are already more than 50 boats on the water, each carrying two or three anglers and a guide. (Although now in June, 50 boats in one section is not as common as it was just a few years ago.) It can be a discouraging sight. The determined dry-fly fisherman just has to make the most of it.

But the Big Hole does offer excellent trout fishing at other times of the year, when the crowds are gone, and when you can count the number of anglers on the river on both hands. Crowded June becomes nearly empty July.

Also, in years when there is a light run-off of snow, the caddisfly hatch can occur prior to the Salmon Fly hatch, from about May 25th to June 25th, offering unmatched early-season dry-fly fishing.

The water conditions on the Big Hole begin to change as summer progresses, with the high water levels dropping, thus making some sections of the river open to wading (though float trips remain popular, especially from the junction of the Wise River down to Melrose). The falling water gives the river's wide, deep pools beautiful definition. It also gives the fly fisherman the opportunity to fish these pools from its wide, open banks rather than from a boat.

The low water during the summer months also opens up some of the upper reaches of the Big Hole to some nice fly fishing for brook trout and grayling between Bryant Bridge and Dicky Bridge.

After the early Salmon Fly hatch, there are not a great many other truly overwhelming hatches on the Big Hole, which allows the innovative fly fisherman to work a great many productive patterns. A number of fly patterns, it turns out, work well on the Big Hole, including Pale Morning Duns, Adams, Royal Wulffs, Trudes, and Troth

Elk-Hair Caddis (#14 to #20). Indeed, enough caddisflies come off the river during the summer months that the caddis patterns, beginning in June, are effective throughout the summer and into the early fall, with the emergence of the giant caddisflies in late summer (imitated by #8 or #10 Giant Orange Sedges).

The Divide to Glen section of the river remains the most productive part of the river throughout the year, at least in terms of big browns and rainbows. A good many six to eight-pound browns are regularly taken from this part of the river, and fish from 16 to 20 inches are common, particularly during the summer evening hatches.

During June and July, dry-fly fishing on the Big Hole can result in 30 fish a day per person.

Any trip to the Big Hole ought to allow, as well, at least one day's fishing along the nearby Wise River, a tributary of the Big Hole, and itself a fine trout stream, heavy with small but challenging and enjoyable fish.

BEAVERHEAD RIVER

Montana

While the Beaverhead is considered among Montana's and the nation's top trout rivers — especially for trophy fish — it has, at best, a checkered history, one marked by serious problems caused mostly by dramatic shifts in river water levels. During the late 1980s the river and its trout habitat suffered dramatically due to drops in water levels. As the river continued to suffer, so did its dominant population of big brown trout. Severe angling restrictions helped, but not as much as rain, a lessening of the ruinous drought situation in southwest Montana, through which the Beaverhead flows. At the apex of the drought in the winter of 1989, the flow on the Beaverhead had been reduced so drastically that state officials estimated that the river had probably lost more than 50 percent of its brown trout population.

Of immediate help in preserving this great trout river was the decision in the late 1980s to release more water from the Clark Canyon Reservoir (which, to a large degree, controls water flow and water levels on the Beaverhead). But even with the additional water coming out of the reservoir, experts predicted that the Beaverhead would need at least two years worth of normal to above-normal rainfall to recover from the ruinous effects of the drought.

It is more than ample testimony to the character of the Beaverhead and its reputation that despite the serious problems it has faced because of the extended drought, it has continued to offer periods of first-rate trout fishing. Today it still remains a trout river of consequence, one of the best brown trout rivers in the world. The bending, open coils of the Beaverhead, its banks often marked by stands of gnarled willows, is a fantastic stream for dry flies, nymphs, and streamers.

South of Twin Bridges, the Beaverhead flows almost straight south toward Dillon and on toward the Clark Canyon Dam and Reservoir. Both the Beaverhead and Ruby rivers break off the Jefferson River above Twin Bridges. While the Beaverhead continues south, the Ruby, another superb Montana trout river, arcs to the northeast before meandering south. To the west of the Beaverhead and the upper channel of the Jefferson are the trout-heavy waters of the Big Hole River.

The Big Hole, Ruby, and Beaverhead rivers have something in common: they are among the most difficult of Montana's trout rivers, demanding and challenging, no matter how skillful a fly fisherman is. Many dry-fly anglers consider the Beaverhead a river without equal, the river they keep coming back to again and again. Both its trout and its beauty are unique and addictive.

The Beaverhead's reputation is based mostly on the numerous trophy-sized brown trout that populate its waters. Fly fishermen coming to the river to try their hand at tempting one of these monsters often do so by employing the local "chuck and duck" technique, which translates into forcing, almost slapping, large streamers along the river's banks, then stripping line and streamer back furiously.

However, fly fishermen are most certainly not limited to the "chuck and duck" approach to the Beaverhead, as the river is rich in nutrients and there are many impressive natural hatches, including caddisflies, craneflies, stoneflies, and Pale Morning Duns. In fact, the Beaverhead River is so rich and abundant in food that the growth rates of its trout may be unmatched on any other trout river in the world. Even with the lingering drought and its damaging effects, the river continues to hold a sizeable number of fish, perhaps more than 2,000 brown trout per river mile.

But dropping water levels on the river have changed the nature of its fishing. Fly fishing the Beaverhead these days takes even more finesse than before, coupled with a willingness to abandon the "chuck and duck" method for more subtle and enticing techniques and approaches. Matching the river's hatches, along with patience and accurate presentations, usually produces not only trout, but trophy-sized trout.

The most important development along the Beaverhead, perhaps as a result of the drought, is the sudden success of nymph fishing (put some extra weight on them; they've got to sink fast to be effective), which probably takes more Beaverhead trout these days than pocketfuls of Woolly Buggers. The Red Squirrel Nymph works well on the Beaverhead, as do the LaFontaine Antron, Cranefly Nymph (#4 to #6), Partridge & Peacock, the T-Bur Stone Nymph, Tim Tollett's Flashback (#10 to #16 — #12 and #14 work best), and stonefly imitations. (There are no large stoneflies in the Beaverhead, but the little yellow/olive ones hatch in the thousands — even the millions.)

Fishing restrictions and limits continue on the Beaverhead River in an effort to protect and preserve the river's magnificent trout, especially since the number of big browns has, unfortunately, dropped by almost 30 percent (that still means more than 100 trout over 20 inches per river mile). Brown trout continue to be the dominant trout on the Beaverhead, composing more than 75 percent of the river's trout population. There are rainbows, and the river holds some very large ones. While the best fish taken from the Beaverhead is a 16 1/2-pound brown, for example, a 15-pound rainbow has also been landed. But the rainbows generally do not come close to the browns, either in size or challenge.

Also, the drought has harmed the Beaverhead's delicate rainbows much more than the brown trout. In some places along the river, especially near the town of Dillon, the proportion of rainbow trout to browns has dropped below five percent. (But the population of rainbows was never high around or below Dillon.)

When water levels are near normal, the Beaverhead below the Clark Canyon Dam can offer excellent fishing from spring into the fall. From April through July is usually an especially good time when caddisflies, Pale Morning Duns, Yellow Stoneflies, and craneflies come off the river in mind-boggling numbers.

A fact that has sort of been held in secrecy for many years is that the Beaverhead has always been a "small fly" fishery. The river has always produced well with small drys and nymphs. (Although the Girdle Bug days are certainly not gone; it's just that the fish have become more and more selective and demand a fly that more closely resembles a caddisfly. However, Girdle Bugs do imitate cranefly larvae very well, and in cranefly hatch and drift periods, the pattern can still draw strikes from huge trout.) But small flies work better, undoubtedly. A local pro, Tim Tollett, reports that most of the large trout (up to seven pounds) he has personally taken off the Beaverhead have fallen to small nymphs — principally to his Flashback pattern — and more than half of that number were taken on a dropper!

The best time to fish the Beaverhead is anytime you can fish. Caddisfly hatches are most prominent in July and August, with August being the best time for evening caddisfly hatches.

Craneflies — which certainly bring up the largest Beaverhead trout — start their hatch about August 20th and continue until about September 15th. Mayfly action starts in April or May; Little Yellow Stoneflies appear from June 20th to July 25th; *Baetis* from around June 20th to July 30th, and then again from September 20th to October 30th; and Pale Morning Duns and caddisflies from July 15th to September 20th.

The Beaverhead is a trout stream that is always changing. From the very first days when its flow of water started from Clark Canyon in 1963, the river's water levels and fishing quality and productivity have gone from one extreme to another. But one thing is certainly true today: the Beaverhead is a river full of large trout, a real western fly-fishing treasure.

HENRY'S FORK OF THE SNAKE RIVER

Idaho

Among the great fisheries of Idaho, one has become so renowned among fly fishermen that many, when they speak of it, speak of it reverently, as though it were truly holy water.

This is the Henry's Fork of the beautiful and powerful Snake River. The river's history is as rich and interesting as its trout. The Snake was an important waterway for the first trappers who entered the mountains. Indeed, Henry's Fork was named for Colonel Andrew Henry of the Rocky Mountain Fur Company. Chased out of Montana by angry bands of Blackfeet Indians, Henry and a small band of trappers moved south out of what would come to be Montana, hastily built a small, rough-hewn fort along the river that now bears Henry's name, and wintered there.

Henry's Lake near the Montana line, below Targhee Pass, and a series of immense springs, called the Big Springs, form the headwaters of Henry's Fork. The springs move an incredible volume of water, more than 150,000 gallons of icy blue-green water a minute, up from among ancient eroded volcanic rock and through great cracks in the surrounding mountain flanks. The trout fishing on Henry's Lake has been as remarkable, at times, as the fishing on Henry's Fork.

Also known as the North Fork of the Snake River, Henry's Fork (and with trout fishermen, it is always Henry's Fork) coils through southeastern Idaho, west of Yellowstone and the wild, breathtaking sprawl of Grand Teton National Park, finally joining the South Fork of the Snake River near the town of Rexburg, Idaho.

The waters of Henry's Fork move out of Big Springs and Henry's Lake into the Island Park Reservoir, which is a

30-mile drive from Yellowstone National Park's west entrance on U.S. Route 191 that follows the river south out of West Yellowstone. Beyond the Osborne Bridge, near Last Chance, river and road run nearly side by side.

Getting to the river is easiest at the Osborne Bridge and at the Railroad Ranch. While it takes more time and effort, the hike to the river from the Box Canyon campground gives you a deeper appreciation of the river's and the land's enduring beauty.

The river's drainage basin sprawls between Henry's Lake and the town of Ashton, encompassing more than 1,000 square miles of high mountain meadow sagebrush country. Although not as well known as the waters of the upper Henry's Fork, the section of the river from its mouth upstream to Ashton offers some excellent fly fishing. For example, in May there is an excellent stonefly hatch downstream of the Vernon bridge.

But when they talk of the Henry's Fork, fly fishermen are usually referring to the upper section of the river, which they divide into two sections — Box Canyon and the lower Mesa Falls (the Warm River, which also offers some excellent trout fishing, joins Henry's Fork below Mesa Falls); and the Railroad Ranch, where the river slows, coils, and widens. There are places where it is more than 250 feet wide, its bright water dimpled by free-rising rainbow trout. Rainbows dominate in the upper sections of Henry's Fork, while on the lower sections of the river there is a healthy population of larger brown trout.

Box Canyon is a narrow, rock-strewn, pinched-in pine valley, where the river rushes hard and fast over galleries of eroding stone for more than three miles. Where it narrows, the river can be 50 feet across or less, while the long sluicing runs can be more than 100 feet wide. Many of the legendary rainbow trout of Henry's Fork have been

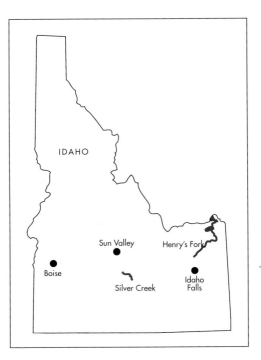

IDAHO

Sun Valley

Henry's Fork

Boise

Idaho Falls

Silver Creek

hooked in Box Canyon, trout that can weigh up to 12 pounds, most taken with large stonefly nymphs or big streamers.

While fly fishing Box Canyon at anytime quickly becomes a cherished memory, coming to the canyon in June for the stonefly hatches is the kind of experience, that rare union of fisherman, river, and insect, that stays with an angler for a lifetime, only improving with time and the passing years.

Henry's Fork widens, slows, changes mood below Box Canyon, as it cuts across the Railroad Ranch and the high country meadows at Last Chance, which is perhaps the most crowded real estate along the river. The river's mood and character change dramatically. The current is softer, the river slower. While streamers and nymphs are still productive along this stretch of the river, the water here was at one time nearly perfect dry-fly water.

This is the section of Henry's Fork that became legendary among fly fishermen, a 12-mile stretch of river flowing from the Island Park Dam downstream to the Railroad Ranch and Last Chance. For more than six miles the Henry's Fork winds through Railroad Ranch. The ranch was originally railroad right-of-way given to the Union Pacific Railroad and its owner, Edward Henry Harriman. In turn, the Harriman family later gave the Railroad Ranch to the people of Idaho. The ranch is now maintained as Harriman State Park.

At its prime, the waters of Henry's Fork were rich and remarkably fecund, marked by thick stands of potamogeton and chara, enduring cycles of insect hatches, many of which came off the river in incredible swarms. This was especially true of sedges and mayflies and the *Ephemerella* flies that would hang like drifting mists just above the surface of the river in early summer and the caddisflies that would spin in the soft wind along the river at twilight. Gray Sedges and Gray-Winged Olives often worked well on Henry's Fork then, as would, when the season and temperature were right, hoppers and ants. Throughout the summer months Pale Morning Duns, Western Green Drakes, Brown Drakes, Tricos, and Mahogany Duns were the most consistently successful flies along most of Henry's Fork, and especially along the broad, open, meandering section of the river that winds through the Railroad Ranch.

Because of the river's great variety and tremendous populations of insects during its glory days, Henry's Fork trout were exceptionally difficult trout to fish for. When it came down to matching the hatch, there was perhaps no more demanding, vexing, thrilling, difficult or enjoyable river than the Snake River's Henry's Fork.

But today, unfortunately, the storied trout populations of the Henry's Fork — particularly in the Railroad Ranch section of the river — no longer exist, due to a host of environmental problems with which the river has been confronted since the 1980s. Very few anglers now even fish the Railroad Ranch section, opting instead for the more productive waters of other western streams such as Montana's Bighorn.

Nevertheless, the Henry's Fork will always remain a favorite U.S. trout river, and is certainly worth a visit by any fly fisherman who has never seen or experienced this legendary water, despite the fact that its fishing potential is currently being so diminished by pollution.

The entire upper run of Henry's Fork, including Box Canyon and the Railroad Ranch, can be fished only with single barbless hooks and artificial lures. Only artificial flies are permitted on that part of the river that is located within the boundaries of the Railroad Ranch. Because the land bordering the river is subject to various land usages — including Harriman State Park and the Harriman Bird Sanctuary — season opening and closing dates, as well as creel limits and fishing regulations, vary considerably from section to section along the Henry's Fork. For example, some sections of the river are open to fishing all year, while others have restricted seasons. So it's best to check with a local source before planning your trip.

For an alternative experience, fly fishermen wanting to sample the beauty of the area around Henry's Fork might want to try the upper reaches of the nearby Fall River, which empties into Henry's Fork near the town of Chester. The lower section of Fall River runs through privately owned property. Like Henry's Fork, there is a wonderful Salmon Fly hatch on Fall River in the early weeks of June.

Rainbow trout between 12 and 15 inches are also common on two of the Henry's Fork other tributaries, Robinson Creek and Warm River. Cranefly and Muskrat Nymphs are as successful on these rivers as they are on Henry's Fork. After the June swarm of Salmon Flies, the best bet here (as well as on the Henry's Fork) are small to medium-sized hoppers.

SILVER CREEK
Idaho

Fly fishing along many of the West's spring or limestone trout creeks and streams is every bit as challenging as, and often tougher than, angling on its larger, faster rivers.

Spring creeks are embedded in the history and evolution of American fly fishing, so much so that many of these creeks are shrouded in a fascinating cloak of angling mysticism. These are the kind of trout rivers that flow through the very heart of the evolution of our fly fishing; the living definition of what many fly fishermen feel is the grand foundation of all fly fishing, the trilogy of fisherman and fish and stream.

The best of the spring creeks seem thriving, maddening, vexing perfections of trout and trout water, the combination of wild fish and wild water that anglers adore and celebrate. The best of them require a high degree of skill. Technically, there is no more demanding trout fishing than on the best spring creeks. And among the very best of the best in Idaho — as well as the world — is Silver Creek. It is a place where, for the skilled (and lucky) angler, the magic and poetry of fly fishing happen.

Fly fishermen from around the world come regularly to Silver Creek to enjoy its beauty and its trout and to test their own prowess, skills. Part of the hailed trout waters of Idaho's Sun Valley, including the equally sublime Big and Little Wood rivers, Silver Creek coils down through basin country, through the high country meadows of southeastern Idaho, 30 miles from the resort town of Sun Valley. The creek has been a mecca for fly fishermen at least as long as Sun Valley has been a mecca for skiers, for more than 50 years, even before the Harriman family developed Sun Valley.

Much like their ranch along the Henry's Fork, the Harriman's initially acquired the Sun Valley land as easement for their Union Pacific Railroad. Once the land was in hand, the family began setting some of it aside as a resort for friends and guests of the railroad. There was pristine trout fishing in the summers and excellent duck hunting and upland bird hunting for pheasant in the fall. Hemingway fell in love with Sun Valley early, and came often for its trout fishing and bird shooting and its deep quiet, wonderful isolation.

The geology and hydrology of Silver Creek are quite unique, even for a blue-ribbon western stream. In character, it is closer to an eastern or British chalkstream than it is to most other western, high country spring creeks. It is full of well-educated, wily, rainbow and brown trout, and conditions along the creek are near perfect for dry-fly fishing for them, from summer well into fall. Silver Creek also has a growing population of brown trout — up to as large as 30 inches — which are taken mostly on streamers. But all but the very largest browns will feed on dry flies, especially terrestrials.

Its famous mayfly hatches are present from opening day (Memorial Day weekend), but increase in intensity and consistency in late June. Fishable hatches continue through the end of the season (the last day in November).

To summarize the hatches: Pale Morning Duns make their appearance from June through July; *Baetis* from June through September; *Callibaetis* (in the slower waters) from June through October; Tricos from mid-July through September; Mahogany Duns (*Paraleptophlebia*) from September to early October; hoppers from mid-July through September; damselflies from July through August; Brown Drakes from the first week in June; and ants and scuds throughout the season.

Aside from these specific hatch imitations, anglers coming to Silver Creek should be armed with a diverse arsenal of fly patterns, including nymphs, emergers, cripples, duns, and spinners.

Angling along Silver Creek is restricted to bank and wading only. No boats are allowed, but certain sections may be fished from a float tube. Many sections of the creek can only be fished with fly rod and artificial flies. The best sections of Silver Creek, the downstream sections, are all catch-and-release water. But there are sections that provide two-fish slot limits (no fish between 12 and 16 inches). The Nature Conservancy, which manages the Silver Creek Preserve, requires fly fishermen to sign in for fishing their water, although there are no rod fees, and access is quite good.

Success here can be a frustrating proposition. But there are some general guidelines for fly fishing difficult spring creeks, even water as demanding as Silver Creek.

First, because it is so easy to become hypnotized by spring creek trout, by their numbers and what seems to be their brazen feeding patterns, you may want to move around a good deal if you can. However, during prime hatch times, this may not be possible, because of the number of anglers on the water, or even necessary, because of the number of fish visible in range of your cast. But, do not get lured into the hopeless situation of wading into a school of feeding trout and thinking that you can tempt them easily, only later to find that you have spent several hours in the same spot without a single strike. Persistence is an asset in fly fishing, of course, but if early on things aren't working right, try moving.

Second, when fishing hatch imitations on this spring creek, do not be a slave to a single fly. Often getting the attention of finicky trout can be as simple as changing flies, either to something that matches a different phase of the ongoing hatch (emergers or spinners, for example), or even tempting the trout with something different. Trying different fly patterns is always advisable when the weather conditions are variable and inconsistent.

Third, only get into the water and wade when necessary, and then wade slowly and carefully.

Fourth (and most important), Silver Creek is a very technical stream. All its fish have Ph.Ds. Success will come readily only to the fly fisherman who knows exactly how to match a hatch and make precise casts, followed by — and this is an imperative — drag-free drifts.

Spring creeks like Silver Creek usually call for long leaders, fine tippets, and small dry flies and nymphs (#16 to #24) fished downstream and across, keeping the sun, whenever possible, off your rod, line, and tippet. Even the most innocent flash may spook spring creek trout. Reach and stop casts work well here.

The heaviest fishing pressure along Silver Creek usually falls between the end of June through Labor Day, but it is a sublime trout stream almost any time of the season.

Overleaf: *The start of the day at Alaska's Bristol Bay Lodge.*

CHAPTER FIVE

THE PACIFIC COAST AND ALASKA

FALL AND SACRAMENTO RIVERS
California

Some of the best fly fishing in the country is to be found in the northern portion of California, which includes such rich and productive watersheds as the Klamath, Eel, Smith, McCloud, Pit, and Upper Trinity rivers; and Lakes Manzanita, Shasta, Lewiston, and Baum. My two favorite rivers in this area are the Fall River, a great trout fishery, and the Sacramento, a great shad and trout fishery.

Fall River

The headwaters of the Fall River begin near Thousand Springs in the Shasta National Forest, west of Big Lake (northeast of Redding, California). Flowing first east, then south, the river is eventually joined by the waters of the Little Tule and Tule rivers in the wide expanse of the great Fall River Valley as the river again bends to the south, flowing toward Fall River Mills.

Fall River is best known for its magnificent hatches of Pale Morning Duns, especially on the upper and middle sections. These hatches come early in the fly-fishing season and remain active along the river for long periods of time. Starting soon after the California trout season opens on the last Saturday in April, the best and most regular and predictable early season hatches occur during May through the latter part of June.

The Pale Morning Dun hatch is sometimes accompanied by an excellent Trico hatch. Fly fishermen working the river early in the morning and again at the end of the day will often be treated to a simultaneous hatch of both flies.

The cooler days of early fall, usually from October until mid-November, again bring Pale Morning Dun and Trico hatches; a third hatch (although somewhat smaller and irregular) of Blue-Winged Olive Duns; and a fourth hatch, an excellent hatch of Big Yellow Mays (*Hexagenia*). As usual, these large mayflies hatch right at dusk and into evening's darkness. All of these hatches give the river a true western feel.

The hatches and the beauty of the river are welcomed every season by the dominant species on the river, rainbow trout, and a few browns. The Fall River rainbows are respectably sized: 12 to 18-inch fish are common.

Good fishing on the Fall River begins as soon as the season opens. During the late spring months, the most productive flies tend to be small Blue-Winged Olive Duns (#20 to #22), Western Green Drakes (#10 to #14), and always, Pale Morning Duns (#16 to #20). As the waters warm, Tricos become increasingly popular (#20 to #24), as do Gray Drakes and light to dark caddisfly patterns (#14 to #18).

Access to much of Fall River can be difficult, as there are only two public access points, one off Island Road by the site of the California Trout organization; the other at the P. G. & E. dredge site, off MacArthur Road. Consequently, most fishermen find it more convenient to fish the river from drift boats.

Sacramento River

A great many of California's rivers rise and flow west from the rugged, massive peaks of the great Sierra Nevada Mountains, including the Sacramento, which has become famous among anglers for its superb shad fishing. The Sacramento's history as a shad fishery did not begin until the 1870s, when the first shad were released into the river. Since then, the Sacramento and two of its tributaries, the Feather and Yuba rivers, have become among the most challenging, productive, and popular shad rivers in North America. Certainly, they are among the West's premier shad fisheries.

Today, shad runs on the Sacramento and its tributaries often swell to incredible numbers of fish. There are years when more than two million shad will crowd these waters. Given such incredible populations, it is common for anglers fishing the Sacramento to take more than 12 fish a day. (Creel limits vary, but the number is usually about 20 shad per angler per day.)

Shad runs into the river normally begin sometime in March, with the fish moving out of San Francisco Bay and into the river slowly, moving as the water temperatures rise. The shad make their big push upriver once the water reaches a steady 65 degrees. This can come at any time from mid-April into May, so that the peak runs usually occur through May and June.

The upper section of the Sacramento, from Redding to the town of Anderson, also provides superb trout fishing. This stretch of river is above the Red Bluff Diversion Dam, which is the upstream limit of the shad run.

In this area, the Sacramento provides a long season of excellent trout fishing, with superb hatches of caddis in the spring and summer, including, in particular, the black *Brachycentrus,* an olive-bodied, gray-winged caddis, and the *Hydropsychidae,* a tan-bodied, gray/brown-winged caddis. Also, for the angler who is willing to fish during the day with a deep-strike indicator, the use of caddis pupa imitations will reward him with rainbows averaging from 14 to 20 inches.

After the spring and summer caddis activity dies down, the spawning activities of Chinook salmon introduce eggs into the stream that trout will gorge themselves on. Egg-pattern fishing will last through most of the winter.

It is also worth noting that because the spawning salmon dislodge many nymphs as they build their spawning redds, those anglers who choose not to fish egg patterns can have equal success with caddis larva or pupa imitations, including *Baetis* nymphs.

One of the great pleasures of the Sacramento River is that it is a river that can be successfully fished from the banks. There is plenty of easy access all along the river, from near Sacramento all the way to the dam. By far the most popular spot along the river is Woodson Bridge Pool, near the town of Corning, at Woodson Bridge State Park. Many fly fishermen prefer to walk the upper river and float the lower sections.

KLAMATH RIVER
California

California has more than 20 steelhead rivers, and the Klamath is generally considered among the best. Steelhead fishermen are drawn to it (and its companion river, the Rogue) year after year because the steelhead begin running in the Klamath earlier than in any of the state's other steelhead rivers. Big returns of one and two-year-old fish, weighing from one to three pounds, make up as much as 95 percent of the fly-caught steelheads on the river. Most of the older steelhead in the Klamath are in the five to 12-pound range. Fish over that size, say in the 20-pound range, are rare.

As they begin their river migration, the steelhead move restlessly through the lower portions of the river below where the Trinity and Klamath join. The Trinity is the largest of the Klamath's tributaries and the steelhead like to gather in the deep cool water at its mouth and along its many smaller feeder creeks and streams.

While water flow plays a big part in the timing of the steelhead run, the Klamath's early run generally picks up steam by August and is a surge by October, the prime month on the river for adult steelhead in the lower Klamath (from the mouth to Weitchpec).

The majority of the larger fish do not get to the Klamath's junction with the Scott River until the last part of October, with the best time being November and December. These winter fish are considerably larger, some reaching as large as 12 pounds. The river will often hold large numbers of these large winter steelhead through the following early spring.

The weather in the fall (late August and October) is usually very mild. Most mornings are cool, with afternoon temperatures in the 70-to-80-degree range. The water temperature at this time of year will be very warm, in the mid-60s to low 70s.

Given its wide differences in countryside, geography, size, and character, the Klamath is easily divided into three distinct sections. The lower river — the more than 40 miles up to Cappell Creek — is rugged, fast, pinched in by steep bluffs. It is largely accessible only by jetboats, of which there are plenty. Today, jetboats have opened the once inaccessible lower Klamath to large numbers of steelhead fishermen.

Between the towns of Johnson (near Cappell Creek) and Orleans, the Klamath River batters through another steep canyon, yet there is access here by way of a road running near the river. The river here is incredibly powerful and brutally clogged with massive rocks and boulders, so that while access can be challenging (indeed as are most accesses by foot on the Klamath), once you get to the water the fishing is easy during the autumn months. However, when fishing the Klamath from Johnson all the way to the mouth of the Trinity near Weitchpec, again most fishermen solve the problem by depending on local guides with jetboats and rafts.

Perhaps the most famous section of the Klamath is the run of water between Orleans to the Iron Gate Dam. This water is renowned for its wonderful fall steelhead run. Most of this section of the river is accessible by way of fairly good roads maintained by the U.S. Forest Service. There is plenty of room for fly fishing here without the need of boats.

The local's knowledge of the river goes a long way on the Klamath, particularly as regards tackle selection. In the old days, local steelheaders used fast-sinking lines almost exclusively. Nowadays floating and sink-tip lines are also employed effectively. Because of the Klamath's high water temperatures, the fish are usually not shy and will come right to the surface to take wet flies (and sometimes drys when the conditions are just right). But during those times when the fish just won't come to the surface (during the mid-part of sunny days, for example), local fly fishermen will switch to sink-tip lines. Later in the season, from late November through January, they will use fast-sinking lines (such as a Teeny T-200 Nymph Line or a sink-tip shooting head), but only after having given the floating line a try.

These fish are not shy, and light tippets are not necessary. Locals routinely use 0X and 1X tippets, using only a lighter one (say a 2X) when fishing dry flies in shallow water.

Barbless hooks are now mandatory, and hook size is limited to a 1/2-inch gape on single hooks.

Like most steelhead, Klamath fish on the run are not finicky eaters. The flies that work well on the river are many, though any selection should include Brindle Bugs with a chenille body, brown hackle and tail; and Silver Hiltons (#6 to #10, and sometimes in the winter, a #4). Other standard steelhead patterns are used, as well as a number of new and highly productive soft-hackle and dry flies that local guides have been designing.

OVERLEAF: *Anglers enjoying the day on one of California's premier trout fisheries, the Fall River.*

In the fall, due to the high water temperatures, once hooked the fish should be played fast and hard. You will find that reviving them — especially the larger ones — will sometimes take quite a while.

The head of the Klamath is truly a different river, because it meanders through true desert country and is greatly affected by the weather. Fishing on this upper section of the river is anything but consistent or even predictable. Fly fishermen visiting the river for the first time and wanting to get a deep and rich sampling of the nature of its steelhead run would be better off sticking to the area below Iron Gate Dam.

While the Klamath and its major tributaries — the Trinity, the Salmon, and the Scott — are known mostly for their steelhead fishing, Chinook salmon do move into these waters. But fishing for them has been significantly curtailed. The entire allowable catch of Chinooks for the entire Klamath-Trinity river system is now only 800 fish per year, and registration regulations are in effect.

You may be aware that it is these Chinooks that are caught in the tangle of a fisheries' controversy, as the local Indian population takes them with nets by the hundreds. The meager population of Klamath Chinooks that do somehow manage to survive the netting are difficult fish, as they are not known for being fly biters. Although the jacks (the two-year old males) are known to take flies very well. If you wish to have a go at these fish, the lower river below its junction with the Trinity is probably the most productive section. The best months for Chinook are August and September. Salmon fishing ends on the river in November.

For the most part, though, fly fishermen travel to the Klamath not for the salmon, but for the river's still healthy and incredible run of steelhead.

UMPQUA AND DESCHUTES RIVERS
Oregon

Following the temptations of the fly rod and the pleasures and challenges of fly fishing take an angler into some of the most spectacularly beautiful country left on the planet, country that still has a wild edge to it.

The big, powerful rivers of the Northwest flow through some truly remarkable high country, among high mountain lakes and vast forest. In Oregon are the fabled waters of the Umpqua and the Deschutes rivers.

Umpqua River

Not far from the high plateau country near Crater Lake and Diamond Lake, the North Branch of the Umpqua muscles its way south, down past Maidu and Lemolo and on to the Pacific. The Umpqua is as rich in angling lore as it is in natural beauty. Many consider it one of the country's best and certainly most famous steelhead river.

The river has been associated with many angling legends. Zane Grey loved the Umpqua and fished it often. (Like so many anglers, Grey stayed at the old Steamboat Lodge, which has become one of the most famous angling lodges in the United States.) The grand tradition of the Steamboat Lodge and the Steamboat steelhead fishermen has continued, even with the creation of the Umpqua National Forest.

One of the best pools along the river is still known as the Kitchen Pool, because it is almost directly under the lodge's kitchen, where the meals are nearly as legendary as the river's steelhead fishing. It was along the rush of the Umpqua that many of what are now considered the classic steelhead flies evolved, including the Gordon, the Green-Butt Skunk, the Stevenson, and the Umpqua Special.

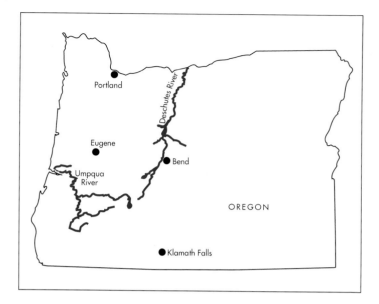

Many fly fishermen still consider the North Umpqua to be the best steelhead river in the country, even though in 1992 and early 1993 the river experienced its lowest runs of summer and winter steelheads in history — estimated at only 1,500 fish compared to its previous 30-year average fish-run population of 10,000 fish per year. Nevertheless (and hopefully once again in average numbers in the future), the celebrated summer-run steelhead begin showing up in the North Umpqua in the spring, and the river bristles with excellent steelhead fishing into October.

The Umpqua is known as much for its challenges as for its beauty. If it is hailed as one of the best steelhead rivers in the world, so it is considered one of the most difficult. It is a fast and powerful watershed, with numerous sections of fast, heavy water as the river roars down through a great conifer forest, through perpetual deep green mists and shadows.

Anglers who return to the Umpqua again and again, year after year, do so as much simply to be on this incredible river as to cast a line for its elusive steelhead.

Deschutes River

The awesome Deschutes River is another story entirely. Rising from headwaters of Little Lava Lake in the rugged peaks of the Cascade mountains in central Oregon, the river winds down past Windigo Pass, flowing through Oregon timber country down to Sun River, where it joins with the Upper Deschutes. Lewis and Clark were probably the first white men to see the Deschutes, and it soon became one of the waterways of the northwestern fur trade. Trappers gave it its name, "the River of Falls."

From the high country, the Deschutes flows into the dry, semi-desert region of Metolius where it is joined by the Crooked River. Where the river flows near the Warm Springs Indian Reservation, between Warm Springs and Maupin, there are populations of wild rainbow trout as well as steelhead. These fish, known as "redsides" because of the brilliant red stripes on their flanks, average from 14 to 18 inches. The prime time to fish for them is during the famous Salmon Fly hatch, which usually runs from mid-May to mid-June.

From here, downstream, to its eventual junction with the Columbia River, the Deschutes is a rough and powerful river, the passion of as many kayakers and rafters as steelhead fishermen.

The Deschutes is a wonderful paradox — a desert river richly alive, teeming with fish, trout and steelhead. Although the Deschutes is a big river and its famous steelhead runs are thick, only the last downstream 100 miles of the river hold migrating steelhead trying to fight their way upstream. Dams and reservoirs along the river have seriously altered the cycles and patterns of steelhead migrations, so that today there is no steelhead migration on the river above the large dam at Warm Springs.

Where the fish continue to run along that last 100 miles of river, however, the steelhead fishing on the Deschutes can be spectacular. This long section of river holds wild Deschutes steelhead, hatchery steelhead, and a scattering of other steelhead populations that move into the river from other tributaries of the Columbia as they try to migrate upstream.

Anglers usually divide the lower Deschutes into three sections: the first beginning upriver at Warm Springs and running down to Maupin, which is among the most difficult sections of the river to fish, with limited access except by raft and drift boat. The next section, from Maupin to Macks Canyon, covering a distance of more than 25 miles, offers better access. There is a road here flanking the east bank of the river for the entire stretch, with numerous access points and campsites.

The last section of the river runs from Macks Canyon to the river's mouth and its union with the Columbia River, east of The Dalles. This stretch of the Deschutes covers more than 20 miles. Easy access to the water again becomes a problem here. About the only solution are rafts, drift boats, and power boats.

Fishing the steelhead runs on the Deschutes is limited to flies and artificial lures. Fly fishermen tend to descend on the river from July through October. The river's summer run of steelhead generally begin showing up at the mouth of the lower Deschutes in early July.

The steelhead run continues through the entire summer and will not complete its cycle until late December. During this period as many as 250,000 steelhead will pass over the Columbia River's Bonneville Dam to begin their upstream migration on the Deschutes, Snake, Salmon, and other rivers in the region.

The Deschutes is especially popular with beginning steelhead fly fishermen, because it offers them a great number of steelhead that can be fished successfully in a wide diversity of ways. Whether you want to try sinking shooting heads or wet flies, or even dry flies, the chances of taking fish are excellent.

Some of the most productive steelhead fly patterns on the Deschutes include the Del Cooper, Juicy Bug, Max Canyon, Green-Butt Skunk, Purple Peril, Rusty Bomber, Black and Purple, Articulated Leech, and Deschutes Demon (#2 to #8).

The species of steelhead of the Deschutes are about equally divided, that is, about half-wild and half-hatchery fish. On average, these are good-sized steelhead, running from five to ten pounds, with the occasional fish in the 12 to 16-pound range.

BRISTOL BAY
Alaska

Alaska often seems an alien country, a great untamed, unspoiled sprawl of wilderness, a wilderness still marked by pristine mountains and rivers, incredible fisheries. Discussing Alaska's premier fishing grounds in detail would take volumes. Even so, for the fly fisherman, any discussion, short or long, would surely include my favorite part of Alaska, the famed waters of Bristol Bay.

Bristol Bay, which lies west of Anchorage, is actually a great stretch of Alaskan coastline along the Bering Sea, extending from the Alaska Peninsula north to Cape Newenham, a distance of almost 200 miles. Bristol Bay is an area as large as the state of Ohio. Yet it is part of an even larger section of Alaska favored by sportsmen for its wildness, especially its fishing. To the north is the massive Alaska Range and the incredibly rich waters of Bristol Bay, while to the south is Shelikof Strait and the Pacific Ocean. Within this vast country is the famous Katmai National Monument, the Brooks River, and the Tikchik region, which cover more than 3,000 square miles of wild country, including many beautiful pristine lakes and rivers. Among the rivers are the hauntingly beautiful Wood, Tikchik, Nushagak, Togiak, Goodnews, and Kvichak rivers, and the Iliamna and Tikchik lakes. The Kvichak River drains Iliamna Lake, the Wood River drains the Wood River lakes, while the Tikchik lakes are drained by the Nushagak River.

Sometime around the second week of June, King (or Chinook) salmon begin their migration up the streams of Bristol Bay, moving through hosts of native trout and Arctic grayling as they move inexorably upstream. The King salmon of Bristol Bay are known both for their numbers and for their size, which is commonly 20 pounds and up, with some salmon reaching 50 pounds.

Bristol Bay is just as famous for its run of sockeye salmon, considered by many to be the largest such run left in the world. The sockeye begin their run in late June or early July when literally millions of sockeye, from five to 10 pounds, fill the streams and rivers.

The sockeye are often followed by smaller humpback (or pink) salmon and chum (or dog) salmon runs.

By mid-August, the silver (or coho) salmon are on the move and they will crowd into the Bristol Bay rivers well into September. Silver salmon, weighing from eight to 15 pounds, are the most popular fly-rod gamefish of the Pacific salmon species that come into Alaska in the sum-

Map labels:

ALASKA

Tikchik River — Nushagak River
Tikchik Lake
Iliamna Lake
Goodnews River
Togiak River
Wood River
Dillingham
Kvichak River
Anchorage

BRISTOL BAY AREA (ALASKA)

mer months to spawn. Silver salmon take flies well, and a fresh fish just out of the ocean is an aggressive fighter and jumper.

Mixed in with these nearly constant salmon runs, the rivers of Bristol Bay are crowded with beautiful rainbow trout, Arctic grayling, and Dolly Varden, all of which are active as the water warms, beginning in June. Mid-summer, late July through mid-August, is an excellent time for dry-fly angling to these species because of the especially good hatches caused by lower water levels and higher water temperatures. Though, throughout the season, Bristol Bay experiences quality insect activity — stone-flies, mayflies, and caddisflies — and the resident fish remain active through the warm Alaskan summer and into the fall, often well into October.

Bristol Bay is wild country, draining hundreds of miles of the best fishing water in Alaska — if not the world — but much of it is accessible only by boat or float plane. For the more adventurous angler, there are many float trip operators plying the rivers of the area. And for those opting for more creature comfort, there are a number of first rate blue-ribbon fly-out lodges in the area, the most famous of which is perhaps the Bristol Bay Lodge, situated on Aleknagik Lake close to the wonderful Agulowak River, which has excellent summer populations of sockeye and Chinook salmon, as well as plenty of rainbow trout, grayling, and char. Coming fast and hard out of the nearby Kilbuck Mountains, the waters of the Goodnews, Kanektok and Togiak are among the last unspoiled native rainbow trout rivers in the world.

If I could have only one fishing trip to Alaska, whether I chose a float trip or fly-outs from a lodge, Bristol Bay is the place I would go for the ultimate Alaskan fishing experience, the place to flood memory with a lifetime's worth of wild beautiful country and wild fish.

APPENDIX

SOURCE LIST FOR LOCAL FLY-FISHING INFORMATION AND TACKLE

Penobscot River

Van Raymond Outfitters
388 South Main Street
Brewer, ME 04412
Contact: Van Raymond
Phone: 207-989-6001
Fax: 207-989-6026

Cape Cod, Cuttyhunk, and Martha's Vineyard

Coop's Bait and Tackle
RFD 19
147 W. Tisbury Road
Edgartown, MA 02539
Contact: Cooper Gilkes
Phone: 508-627-8202

Housatonic River

Joe Garman
887 Main Street
Manchester, CT 06040
Phone: 203-643-2401

Valley Angler
56 Padanasam Road
Danbury, CT 06811
Contact: Scott Bennett
Phone: 203-792-8324
Fax: 203-790-7387

Long Island Sound

Urban Angler, Ltd.
206 5th Avenue Third Floor
New York, NY 10010
Contact: Jon Fisher
Phone: 800-255-5488
Fax: 212-473-4020

Beaverkill River

Fur, Fin, & Feather
109 Debruce Road
Livingston Manor, NY 12758
Contact: Richard or Sue Post
Phone: 845-439-4476

Beaverkill Angler
P.O. Box 198
Stewart Avenue
Roscoe, NY 12776
Contact: Budge Loekle
Phone: 607-498-5194

Delaware River

Anglers' Pro Shop
224 Bethlehem Pike
Souderton, PA 18964
Contact: Bill Hayes
Phone: 215-721-4909

A.A. Outfitters
HC1 Box 1030
Blakeslee, PA 18610
Contact: Gene Ercolani
Phone: 570-643-8000

Juniata River

Clouser's Fly Shop
101 Ulrich Street
Royalton, Middletown, PA
17057
Contact: Bob Clouser
Phone: 717-944-6541

Susquehanna River

Clouser's Fly Shop
(see *Juniata River*)

Gunpowder Falls River

On The Fly
538 Monkton Road
Monkton, MD 21111
Contact: Rick Martin
Phone: 410-821-8938

Potomac River

The Angler's Lie
2165 North Glebe Road
Arlington, VA 22207
Contact: Newell Steele
Phone: 703-527-2524
Fax: 703-430-4495

South Fork of the Shenandoah River

The Angler's Lie
(see *Potomac River*)

Rapidan River and Mossy Creek

Murray's Fly Shop
121 Main Street
P.O. Box 156
Edinburg, VA 22824
Contact: Harry Murray
Phone: 703-984-4212
Fax: 703-984-4895

James River

Stoney Creek Tackle
188 Zan Road
Seminole Square
Charlottesville, VA 22901
Contact: Tim Merrick
Phone: 804-973-5151

Lake Okeechobee

Lehr's Tackle Shop
1366 N. Tamiami Trail
North Ft. Myers, FL 33903
Contact: Dave Westra
Phone: 813-995-2280

Ten Thousand Islands

Capt. Harry's Fishing Supply
100 N.E. 11th Street
Miami, FL 33132
Contact: Carl Liederman
Phone: 305-374-4661
Fax: 305-374-3713

Lehr's Tackle Shop
(see *Lake Okeechobee*)

Florida Keys

World Wide Sportsman
P.O. Box 787
Islamorada, FL 33036
Contact: George Hommell
Phone: 305-664-4615
Fax: 305-664-3692

White and Norfork Rivers

Blue Ribbon Flies
P.O. Box 1080
960 Highway 5 South
Mountain Home, AR
72653
Contact: Dale Fulton
Phone: 870-425-0447

Au Sable and Pere Marquette Rivers

The Fly Factory &
Ray's Canoeing
P.O. Box 709
200 Ingham
Grayling, MI 49738
Contact: Steve Southard
Phone: 989-348-5844

Gates' Au Sable Lodge
471 Stephan Bridge Road
Grayling, MI 49738
Contact: Rusty Gates
Phone: 989-348-8462

Johnson's Pere Marquette
River Lodge
Rt. 1, Box 1290

M37 South
Baldwin, MI 49304
Contact: Jim Johnson
Phone: 616-745-3972

Roaring Fork and Frying Pan Rivers

Roaring Fork Anglers
2114 B Grand Avenue
Glenwood Springs, CO
81601
Contact: Carl Maulbetsch
Phone: 970-945-0180

Taylor Creek Fly Shops
P.O. Box 799
City Market Shopping Ctr.
Basalt, CO 81621
Contact: Bill Fitzsimmons
Phone: 970-927-4374

Green River

Angler's Inn
2292 Highland Drive
Salt Lake City, UT 84106
Contact: Susan Hanson
Phone: 801-466-3921
Fax: 801-483-1885

Yellowstone National Park

Blue Ribbon Flies
305 Canyon Street
West Yellowstone, MT 59758
Contact: Craig Mathews
Phone: 406-646-7642
Fax: 406-646-9045

Bud Lilly's Trout Shop
39 Madison Avenue
P.O. Box 698
West Yellowstone, MT
59758
Contact: Jim Criner
Phone: 406-646-7801 or
800-854-9559
Fax: 406-646-9370

Bighorn River

Bighorn Angler
Box 7578
Ft. Smith, MT 59035
Contact: Mike Craig
Phone: 406-666-2233

Yellowstone River - Beyond the Park

Dan Bailey's Fly Shop
209 West Park Street
P.O. Box 1019
Livingston, MT 59047
Contact: John Bailey
Phone: 406-222-1673 or
800-356-4052
Fax: 406-222-8450

George Anderson's
Yellowstone Angler
Highway 89 South
P.O. Box 660
Livingston, MT 59047
Contact: Brant Oswald
Phone: 406-222-7130
Fax: 406-222-7153

Montana's Master Angler
Fly Shop
602 12th Street
Livingston, MT 59047
Contact: Tom Travis
Phone: 406-222-2273

Madison River

Blue Ribbon Flies
(see *Yellowstone National Park*)

Bud Lilly's Trout Shop
(see *Yellowstone National Park*)

Missouri River

Montana Fly Goods
2125 Euclid
Helena, MT 59601
Contact: Garry Stocker
Phone: 406-442-2630 or
800-466-9589

Big Hole River

Frontier Anglers
680 N. Montana Street
P.O. Box 11
Dillon, MT 59725
Contact: Tim Tollett
Phone: 406-683-5276 or
800-228-5263
Fax: 406-683-4216

Beaverhead River

Frontier Anglers
(see *Big Hole River*)

Henry's Fork of the Snake River

Last Chance Lodge &
Outfitters
3350 Highway 20
Island Park, ID 83429
Contact: Philip Chavez
Phone: 800-428-8338

Bud Lilly's Trout Shop
39 Madison Avenue
P.O. Box 698
West Yellowstone, MT 59758
Contact: Jim Criner
Phone: 406-646-7801 or
800-854-9559
Fax: 406-646-9370

Silver Creek

Silver Creek Outfitters
507 N. Main Street
Ketchum, ID 83340
Contact: Peter Crow
Phone: 208-726-5282 or
800-732-5687
Fax: 208-726-9056

Fall and Sacramento Rivers

The Fly Shop
4140 Churn Creek Road
Redding, CA 96002
Contact: Andy Burk
Phone: 530-222-3555 or
800-669-3474
Fax: 530-222-3572

Klamath River

The Fly Shop
(see *Fall/Sacramento Rivers*)

Umpqua/Deschutes Rivers

Deschutes River Outfitters
61115 S. Highway 97
Bend, OR 97702
Contact: Greg Price
Phone: 541-388-8191
Fax: 541-388-4509

Bristol Bay

Bristol Bay Lodge
(October 1 - June 1)
2422 Hunter Rd
Ellensburg, WA 99576
Phone: 509-964-2094
Fax: 509-964-2269

(June 1 - September 30)
P.O. Box 1509
Dillingham, AK 99576
Phone: 907-842-2500
Contact: Ron McMillan

INDEX

FLY PATTERNS AND HATCHES

Hatches